Money

Bare Basic Facts

Personal Financial Education

For my mother

Money

Bare Basic Facts

Personal Financial Education

Sarah Oliver

Tarquin Publications

© Sarah Oliver 2009

Cover illustration by Sarah Oliver

Published by
Tarquin Publications
99 Hatfield Road
St Albans AL1 4JL
UK

www.tarquinbooks.com

ISBN 978 1 89961 882 8

Design by Free Thinking Design

Printed in Malta by Melita Press

Acknowledgements

The author and publisher wish to thank the following for their kind advice, information and permissions in compiling this book.

Jim McCartan, Detective Inspector, Specialist Fraud Unit, Lothian and Borders Police

Hasbro for images from MONOPOLY @ 2008 Hasbro. Used with permission.

Cambridge University Press for definitions taken from the Cambridge Advanced Learner's Dictionary, 2nd edition, (2005). For more definitions see http://dictionary.cambridge.org/

To the following for the permission use of their logos:

AIB	HSBC
American Express	Maestro
APACS	Mastercard
BACS	Norwegian Post
Bank of England	Royal Mail UK
Bank of Scotland	Solo
Barclays	Standard Chartered
Calyon / Crédit Agricole	Standing Order
CIB	Swedish Post
Credit Swiss	Switch
Danish Post	Thomas Cook
Direct Debit	Visa
German Post	

About this Book

I was inspired to write this book by a conversation I had with my teenaged godson Daniel, who asked "How come you get 'interest' but you also have to pay it?"

The resulting book is for everyone starting to be independent, and for adults unsure about banking and financial systems, as well as for those who need reminders of how everyday finance works.

It need not be read in sequence. Dip in to any subject. Each section stands alone.

To find a topic, search in the contents at the front of the book. To look up financial terms, refer to the index at the back of the book.

Words in purple indicate that there is a whole section about that matter. Simply look for it in the index at the back of the book.

Written straightforwardly, it explains how to manage your own money. Short definitions and lucid information make money administration clear and simple.

Everything is just really useful down-to-earth practical information.

Sarah Oliver

Money

Bare Basic Facts

Personal Financial Education for Young People

Chapter 1 Money

Chapter 2 Banks

Chapter 3 Borrowing

Chapter 4 Getting Money

Chapter 5 Keeping Money

Chapter 6 Losing Money

Chapter 7 Paying Money

Chapter 8 Moving Money

Chapter 9 Money Abroad

1. Money

1.1 Money

Describes and defines.

> Money is the coins or notes [bills], which are used to buy things, or the amount of these that one person has.

Old money

New money

Monopoly money

Slang words for money:

Rich or poor there are many different words for **money**, such as: beans, brass, bread, dosh, doubloons, dough, lolly, loot, matza, mazuma, moolah, oscar, rhino, spondulicks, wedge, wonga...

mega bucks = a huge quantity of **money**

wad = a large amount of **money** for spending on enjoyment

a packet = a sizable amount of **money**

peanuts = a trifling amount of **money**

shrapnel = loose change

folding money = notes not coins

readies = cash in hand "ready" to spend

costa mint & costa bomb = expensive

a snip = cheap, a bargain

quid, nicker, sovs = pound(s) £   buck, greenback = USdollar $

Euros = are so new that they are just €uros.

5 = fiver,   10 = tenner,   100 = one-er/ a ton,   1,000 = a grand.

Money Phrases

danger money (called "hazardous-duty pay" in North America)
is extra **money** that is paid to someone because their job is dangerous.

easy money
money that is easily and sometimes dishonestly earned

good money
an amount of **money** that you think is large: *I paid good money for it.*

hush money
money that is given to someone to make them keep something they know secret. Blackmail: *She claimed that the government minister had offered her hush money to keep the scandal a secret.*

key money

a payment demanded by the owner of a house, apartment or shop from the person who is going to rent it Sometimes called "a deposit".

to launder money

to move **money** which has been obtained illegally through banks and other businesses to make it seem to have been obtained legally: **Money** laundering is a way of hiding money obtained from illegal drugs or other criminal activities.

money in something

If you say that there is **money** in something, you mean that the activity will produce a profit: *There's money in it for you.*

money is tight / short

not to have much **money** (usually temporary)

money well spent SAYING

money spent on something worth while: *I had some very expensive dental treatment recently - but it was money **well spent** - it'll save me problems in the future.*

moneyed

rich, a moneyed family

money-grubbing DISAPPROVING

Someone or something that is money-grubbing has **money** as their main interest and does anything they can to get lots of it.

money market

the system in which banks and other similar organizations buy and sell **money** from each other

money supply

all the **money** which is in use in a county

protection money

money that criminals take from people in exchange for agreeing not to hurt them or damage their property

put your money where your mouth is INFORMAL

to show by your actions and not just your words that you support or believe in something

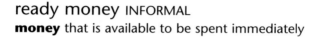

put money into something

invest in something

ready money INFORMAL

money that is available to be spent immediately

seed money

money used to start a development or activity

spending money

money that you can spend for fun, entertainment, personal things, etc: *How much spending money are you taking on holiday?*

the smart money

money that is invested by experienced investors who know a lot about what they are doing: *The smart money is coming back into mortgages as the best investment now.*

the money is good SAYING

the amount of pay is high

money for old rope (ALSO money for jam)

money you get for doing something very easy: *Babysitting is money for old rope if the children don't wake up.*

have money to burn

to spend a lot of **money** on things that are not necessary.

see the colour of somebody's money

To see the colour of someone's **money** is to make certain that a person is going to pay for something.

throw good money after bad

to waste **money** by spending more **money** on something that you have already spent **money** on and which is no good.

1. Money

1.2 Cash

What it is. When to use it. Risks. Definitions.

> **Cash** is real physical money - the stuff you can touch; not cheques and not plastic cards.
>
> **Cash** is the coins and notes in your pockets, wallets and purses.

Small shops and businesses normally use **cash**. For example if you're buying chocolate you are unlikely to pay with a plastic card.

For bigger amounts of money, for example if you are buying a bicycle or a car, you will be able to pay either with **cash**, a cheque or with a plastic card.

Larger businesses are more likely to accept payment made with credit or debit cards, or cheques.

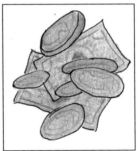

If people ask whether you can pay **cash**, what they might really be trying to find out is whether you can pay them in notes and coins so that they do not have to issue a receipt, hence they do not have to declare your purchase to the tax authorities. Sometimes small businesses ask for **cash**, simply because it is easier for them to process without bothering to go to a bank.

Cash transactions are more difficult to trace. So if you think you will ever have to prove that you bought something, for example if you have to take something back to the shop to be repaired or replaced, then make sure that you ask for a receipt.

To **cash** a cheque means to get money in your hand from a cheque, through a bank.

Cash Phrases

cashless
using or operating with credit and debit cards and electronic systems, not money in the form of coins or notes

cash card (USA ATM card)
a special plastic card given to you by a bank, that allows you to take money out of your bank account using a cash machine.

cash desk
the place in a shop where you can pay for the things that you buy

cash flow
the amount of money moving into and out of a business

cash machine (USA ATM, AUSTRALIAN ENGLISH automatic teller machine)
Cash dispenser. A machine, usually in a wall outside a bank, from which you can take money out of your bank account using a special card

cash register
A machine in a shop or other business that records sales and into which money received is put

e-cash
money from a special bank account which is used to buy goods and services over the Internet by sending information from your computer

hard cash
money in the form of coins or notes but not cheques or a credit card

petty cash
a small amount of money kept in an office for buying cheap items

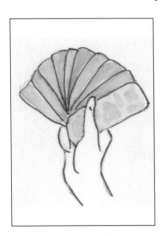

cash up
to count all the money taken by a shop or business at the end of each day

consumer
a person who buys goods or services for their own use

consumerism
1 the state of advanced industrial society in which a lot of goods are bought and sold
2 DISAPPROVING when too much attention is given to buying and owning things.

THINK TWICE

A **consumer** has a choice: buy or do not buy. Try not to allow fashion or advertisements pressurise you into buying something that you don't particularly want or need. One more thing is *not* going to change your life.

1. Money

1.3 How Much to Spend

It's in your control.

> ### THINK TWICE
>
> **NEVER spend more money than you have.**
>
> *"Annual income twenty pounds, annual expenditure nineteen nineteen six, result happiness.*
>
> *Annual income twenty pounds, annual expenditure twenty pounds ought and six, result misery."*
>
> Mr. Micawber, *David Copperfield*, CHARLES DICKENS

This means:

If your income is £20.00 and your expenditure is £19.99
– the result is happiness...

BUT

If your income is £20.00 and your expenditure is £20.01
– the result is misery...

> Live within your means, that is, what you spend has to be less than what you earn. Income must be more than expenditure, if not, you'll get into debt.

In other words, don't overspend – even by one penny.

Unfortunately money doesn't grow on trees.

You have to work to get it.

Keep control over your money.

If you don't, it'll drift away.

2. Banks

2.1 Banks

**Banks and building societies. What are they.
What do they do. Different kinds.**

> **Banks** are business organizations where people and businesses can invest or borrow money, change it to foreign money..., or a building where these services are offered.

Piggy **banks** are fine for saving coins.

BUT... cash boxes can be stolen; even safes can be broken into.

  Don't stuff a mattress with money. It's not a safe place.

Once you start to earn more money, it's best to put it into a **bank**.

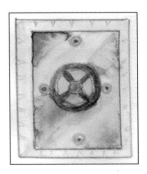 A **bank** vault is the safest place for your money.

THINK TWICE

Even if you leave your money in a **bank account** for a long time it is still your money. It does not belong to the **bank**.

Banks have to pay for the buildings they work in and the people who work in them, so **banks** have to make money. They do this by charging customers fees for various different services, and particularly by charging interest for lending money.

THINK TWICE

REMEMBER – **Banks** are *not* public services.

Banks are businesses that want to make money. **Banks** need customers. They will make their offers sound very attractive, even give away gifts and offer other incentives to entice you to join them. They advertise on TV, radio, the internet, in newspapers and magazines, making their loans and fees sound glamorous. But a cost is not cool, it's just a cost. People who work in **banks** get paid a commission fee or bonuses every time a customer agrees to borrow money. **Banks** want you to use their services, so that they can charge you for them. Once you have got a bank account, **banks** will try to make you take out loans, that is, to borrow money, because they will then be able to charge you interest, and make money from you.

THINK TWICE

Banks make borrowing money very easy, but BEWARE, paying back money that you have borrowed is MUCH MORE DIFFICULT. **Banks** make it easy to get into debt. This is one of the ways that they make money.

Don't choose the first **bank** you come across, because it may not be the most suitable for you. Compare and contrast them. Look carefully at what they offer and ask yourself... "Is this what I need?"

There is no point in being loyal to a **bank**. If one **bank** doesn't offer you what YOU need, ask another. As your circumstances change, find out what other **banks** can offer you. Do not hesitate to change **banks**, if they can offer you the service you want at a better price, efficiently. Choosing a **bank** is just like buying anything else, find out what you get for trusting them with your money, and find out exactly how much it costs.

Bank phrases

A savings bank
offers accounts where your money earns interest.

merchant banks
have companies as customers rather than individuals.

bankable
means likely to make money.

bankability
is an ability to make money.

A clearing bank
exchanges cheques with other **banks** through a central organization called a clearing house, which is a central office used by **banks** to collect and send out money and cheques.

A central bank
provides services to national governments, puts official financial plans of that government into operation, and controls the amount of money in countries' economies. The Bank of England is the Central Bank of the UK.

To break the bank

is a light-hearted expression meaning: doesn't cost too much.
"£2 won't break the bank!"

A building society

is a kind of savings **bank**. Sometimes they're called "Savings and Loan Associations". They focus on long term savings, and some also have cheque books and cash machine cards. Building societies take deposits from customers, on which interest is paid. They lend money to borrowers, mainly in the form of mortgage loans for buying houses.

The World Bank

The World Bank is an international organisation which was formed in 1945 to help economic development, especially of poorer countries.

The World Bank is not an ordinary bank. It works as an international development organisation that provides funding to help improvement in poorer countries in all sorts of spheres of life, such as agriculture, infrastructure, education, social services, employment, government and business.

2. Banks

2.2 Bank Accounts

**What they are. How they work. Different kinds.
How to select. Pros & cons.**

> A **bank account** is an arrangement with a bank that allows a bank to keep your money, in such a way that you may take it out or put more in, according to their rules.

There are *many* different kinds of **bank accounts**.

Banks encourage people to open **accounts**.

The more people who open **accounts** the more money **banks** earn.

You have to choose the **accounts** that are MOST SUITABLE FOR *YOU*.

To do this, ask 3 or 4 different banks what **bank accounts** they can offer you. Compare them, and ask family or friends *then* decide which to choose.

Which bank account is best?

Different kinds of **bank accounts** have different advantages and disadvantages as well as different rules (conditions) attached to them. Such as **accounts** that:

- require that customers keep a *minimum balance* in the **account**.
- charge a *monthly service charge* even if you do not use the services. If you use bank services a lot, it might be worth it, otherwise choose an account with no monthly fee.
- use *passbooks* but not cheques or bank cards - these **accounts** are good for people who want to put small or medium amounts of cash into their bank irregularly.

- offer comparatively *higher interest* if you leave your money for a *longer set time* in the bank, but you CANNOT TOUCH YOUR MONEY AT ALL during the agreed time limit.
- *limit* the number of cheques, withdrawals, deposits and ATM uses each month.
- are for *two people*. These are called *joint accounts* and are sometimes used by married couples.

Account phrases

THINK TWICE

Ask questions. Don't hesitate. Banks will tell you their conditions.

Then YOU decide which accounts are best for YOUR OWN individual financial situation.

Current Accounts [checking accounts] are for ordinary daily use.

These kinds of **accounts** give you a cheque book and a plastic card, so you can write cheques, get money from an ATM (cash-machine) using a bank card and get salaries paid directly into the **account**, BUT they do not usually give much interest.

Deposit Accounts [savings accounts] pay interest.

Money can be left in them for a long time. There are several different kinds of **deposit accounts**. Find out what interest rate they offer. It is usually better than in current **accounts**. Some of these **accounts** insist that you leave your money in them untouched for a very long time, and if you break this agreement by withdrawing your money before the time is up, then you will have to pay the bank an amount as a penalty. Look at the rules (conditions) and the interest rate carefully before opening this kind of **account**.

On-line / internet accounts

These are **bank accounts** that can be accessed only on the net (World Wide Web). **On-line accounts**, or **internet accounts** usually offer higher interest rates, even on small balances: around 5% for current accounts.

THINK TWICE

BEWARE – in spite of strenuous efforts by banks' computer specialists to make these **accounts** secure, **on-line accounts** are still prone to fraud, because all computer systems are hack-able. Even so-called "secure" government computer systems, which have been skilfully encrypted at considerable expense, have been broken into. As the risk of fraud is greater with **internet/on-line accounts** than with others, people with **on-line accounts** tend to log-on every few days to check that there are no unknown transactions in their accounts.

Anything on-line
could be hacked

An "**expense account**" has nothing to do with banks: it is an arrangement in which your employer will pay for some things that you need to buy while doing your job.

2. Banks

2.3 Account Number

What it is. What it's for. How to handle it

This is a unique number given to each individual bank account. The bank **account number** identifies who the account belongs to.

The **bank account number** and the sort code and the name of the bank all together make a kind of "financial address".

These 3 pieces of information show exactly where your bank account is.

You will find your **account number** on debit and credit cards, and on cheque books and statements. On your statement you may also find an IBAN number, which is required in order to send and receive money between countries.

THINK TWICE

Do not leave this information lying around.

It is to be given *only* to people who need it for a known purpose.

If people ask for this information, find out why they want to know it, and if you are in ANY doubt, just don't give it to them.

NEVER give it over the telephone, unless *you* have telephoned your bank. If someone telephones claiming to be calling from a bank, it is a fraudster trying to steal your financial identity, so, do not give any information, because no real bank ever telephones to ask for your **account number**.

If you have a job, you may have to give this information to the people you work for, that is, your employers, so that they can pay you with the direct credit method.

BANK ACCOUNT IDENTIFICATION NUMBERS

2. Banks

2.4 How to Open a Bank Account

**How to do it. When to do it. What you need.
Different kinds.**

It is quite a complicated process opening a **bank account**. You will have to fill-in an application form. Many **banks** have special rules for young people and for students.

> All banks have very strict rules, and will insist on seeing:
>
> 1. documents to prove who you are – "ID Verification"
> 2. documents to prove where you live – "Address Verification"

Most banks offer different **bank accounts** to children, young people and to students. Usually they offer basic **bank accounts** to children from the age of about 11.

If you are *under 11 years old:*

Your parents or guardians can **open a bank account** for you from the moment you are born. They can give you:

– a savings account that has no cheques or credit cards. It has a passbook, which gets updated each time you, or anyone else goes to the bank to withdraw or deposit money.

Or

– a "trustee account" which is one that is for children but is entirely controlled and operated by the parents or legal guardians on behalf of the child, but not by the child, who, alone, cannot touch the money.

If you are *between 11 and 17 years old:*

You can open a bank account if you go to the bank with a parent or guardian who must have:

- proof of the adult's identity - A passport, birth certificate or photograph driving licence.

- proof of the adult's address - A utility bill (electricity, telephone, gas or water bill) showing the adult's name and address.

- proof of the young person's identity: a passport or birth certificate.

A young person's bank account does not offer a chequebook or a credit card. You can get a basic debit card, which has no cheque guarantee on it. You can use it to withdraw money.

You can open some kinds of **accounts** with a deposit of £1. You cannot borrow money. So: no credit cards, no overdrafts, no loans.

You can set up direct debits, but only *if* you have enough money in your account, and can prove that you will continue to have enough to be able to afford it.

Even at this stage, you have a financial identity. Your parent or guardian should guard it carefully, so as to prevent identity fraud.

Once you are *18 years old*, everything changes, because in Britain legally you become an adult. In some other countries the age is 21.

Each bank has its own rules. Most banks offer special **accounts** to young people under 20, and to students.

If you are opening a Student Account, you must provide evidence that you will be a student. This means a letter of acceptance from your University or College, and a letter from the University Central Admissions Service - UCAS, or from a student loan company, or from a Students' Award Agency. If you already have a photograph student card, take it with you when you go to a bank to open an account.

As soon as you are legally an adult, credit companies are allowed to try to sell you credit cards and banks may send you leaflets outlining the benefits of borrowing and trying to persuade you to take out various loans. They want to make money, which they do from the interest they charge on loans.

OPENING A BANK ACCOUNT

If you earn money regularly and can prove it by having a salary regularly paid into your account over several months, and can show reputable lenders [banks or building societies] that you are responsible with money, then you are likely to be able to get a credit card. Some special Student **Bank Accounts** will allow you to borrow money, if you sign an undertaking to pay a minimum amount of the agreed loan every month. There are rigorous rules about this and penalties for failure to pay. Make sure that you read the bank's conditions thoroughly.

If you do not yet earn much money it is unlikely that banks will offer you a credit card immediately, unless someone agrees to "stand guarantor" for you. See section on guarantors.

A guarantor is someone with a long and reliable credit history, whose good financial record is accepted by banks as a guarantee that the loan will be paid back. This person is likely to be a parent or guardian and usually they do this for major loans such as for a mortgage to buy a house.

To decide which bank and what kind of bank account is BEST FOR YOU, see the section on bank accounts chapter 2.3.

THINK TWICE

REMEMBER – As soon as you open a bank account, you will have a financial identity.

GUARD IT – Keep all the account numbers and pin numbers safe.

NEVER tell anyone what they are.

THINK TWICE

BEWARE – From this point onwards in your financial life, you start your own personal financial record or credit score. From now on, all your financial life is dependent on having a good credit history. See sections on credit history at chapter 3.7 and on debt chapter 6.1.

YOU have to "manage" your own money – the bank will not do it for you...

2. Banks

2.5 Financial Guarantor

What they are. What they do. What you have to do.

> A **financial guarantor** is an organisation or person who is willing to guarantee to a lender that a loan will be paid back. **Financial guarantors** take on formal responsibility for borrowers' actions.

A **financial guarantor** believes that you will not get into debt. A **financial guarantor** gives his/her own name to lenders, and by doing so agrees *in principal* to pay off the debt *if* you do not. However, **financial guarantors** do not intend to pay the debt themselves.

Financial guarantors might be parents, guardians, other relatives or financial trusts that help you to get a loan by convincing the lender that you are reliable and will pay back your debt, on time. They do this by telling the lender that you are of good character and that they will be responsible to pay your debt for you, *if* you fail to pay it.

THINK TWICE

Borrowers can ask people to "**stand guarantor**" for them. Some people will not agree to **stand guarantor** for anyone. If someone does agree to **stand guarantor** legally for you, this does NOT mean that they intend to pay your debt for you.

A responsible young man

If you default on a loan (do not pay it back on time) and your financial guarantor pays the lender for you, THE DEBT STILL EXISTS, and *you will then owe* your **financial guarantor** the amount s/he has had to pay for you.

THINK TWICE

You must still pay your debt. There is no way out of paying back debts.

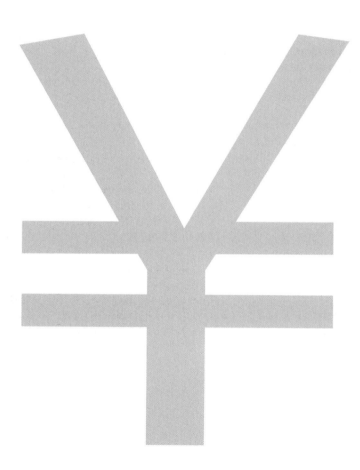

Banks

2. Banks

2.6 Cash Machines

What they are. How they work. Potential problems.

Hole-in-the-wall banks sometimes called **Auto-tellers** or **ATMs**

ATM stands for: automatic teller machine.

Cash machines /dispensers are usually open all day and all night.

You need a PIN to use a cash-machine.

A PIN is your secret code number.

Cash-machines are for withdrawing money from banks. Read the screen with care. Do not be put off by people being impatient behind you.   Follow the on-screen instructions. Try not to use **ATMs** at night in dark places – go somewhere well lit with people around. Do not use any **ATM** that looks odd, or has unusual screen messages. It may mean that it has been tampered with by thieves planning to steal your money. Consider taking a friend with you when you use **ATMs** so that one of you can look out for "shoulder surfers".

 **THINK TWICE**

BEWARE – Watch out for thieves watching you

"Shoulder surfers" look over your shoulder when you enter your PIN. They try to find out your PIN number. Shield the key-pad with your body so that your PIN cannot be seen. If someone is  standing too close, politely ask them to move further away; only thieves would object. Cover the key-pad with one hand while entering your PIN with the other.

If anyone interrupts you, no matter how innocently, do not let go of your card. Take your money and your card *before* looking up or turning away from the **cash machine**. This is because thieves can work in pairs: while one distracts you, the other grabs your card and takes your money.

- Stand close to the **ATM**, so any cameras behind you cannot record your PIN.
- Remember – mobile phones can have cameras in them.
- As soon as your card pops out of the **cash machine [ATM]**, quickly put it away.
- Take your money without delay and *immediately* put it away safely.
- Make sure that you've done all this *before* moving away from the **cash machine**.
- Do not let a stranger help you to use the **ATM**.

Sometimes robbers will watch where people put their cash, then follow them and try to steal it. Thieves observe people withdrawing money from **ATMs**, so:

BE AWARE BE ALERT THIEVES ARE ABOUT.

Ignore any beggars nearby. If they are really too close, aggressive or intimidating, simply go to another machine.

THINK TWICE

BEWARE – Some **cash machines** charge a fee for *each* use. They can be expensive. Usually your own bank will not charge you to use their **cash machines**, but other **cash machines** operated by private companies will charge. The screen will tell you if you will NOT be charged, otherwise *assume that you will be charged.*

Banks put limits on the amount of money that can be withdrawn from **ATMs** per day. The limits are between £200 and £500, and usually less for teenagers.

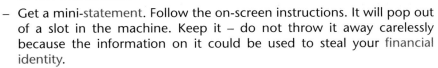

You can use **cash machines** to:

- Withdraw up to the limit allowed if you have that amount in your account.
- Check your balance. To do this, follow the on-screen instructions.
- Get a mini-statement. Follow the on-screen instructions. It will pop out of a slot in the machine. Keep it – do not throw it away carelessly because the information on it could be used to steal your financial identity.
- Pay some kinds of bills. This has to be set up in advance through your bank and with the companies to which you plan to pay bills – usually for utility bills.
- Transfer money. This has to be set up in advance through your bank and pre-selecting the account numbers to which you plan to transfer money.
- Deposit money. Not all **ATMs** offer this service. Follow the on-screen options. An envelope will pop out of the **cash machine** into which you put your money [not coins], write the information asked for on the outside, then put the envelope back through the slot in the **ATM**. Later, the money will be deposited by bank staff. Allow 4 working days for deposits made in this way to reach the specified account.

THINK TWICE

Always cover the key-pad with one hand while you enter your PIN with the other.

THINK TWICE

BEWARE – The surface of **ATMs** should be completely smooth with nothing stuck on it.

Look for any irregularities on the surface of **ATMs**, because:

- Small cameras can be hidden in strips that look like the surface of the **ATM**. They can be stuck with double sided tape onto the top on an **ATM**, so that it photographs your fingers entering your PIN. Some of them can even relay your PIN to a data collector not far away. You don't even know that you have been scammed.
- Any information about an **ATM** will be on screen. If there is an "Out of Order" sign stuck onto an ATM, beware because it may have been put by thieves who are trying to steer you towards another **ATM** where they are operating a scam. If an **ATM** is *really* out of order – it will say so, on screen.

One scam to watch out for works like this:

A thin sheet of clear plastic is cut so that it is less than a millimeter longer than a credit or debit card, and exactly the same width. It is then put into the card slot in an **ATM**. There is such a very small part of it showing that it cannot be seen by customers unless they look very closely indeed. However, the very edge of the thin piece of plastic can be felt if you run a thumb over the slot. *Do this before using ATMs*. If there is anything sticking out of the card slot, remove it, or, if you cannot, then do not use that **ATM**, and report it to the bank.

Customers who have not noticed the **ATM** has been tampered with, put in their cards:

- if the card goes *under* the plastic it gets stuck in the **ATM**. Just then, a nice middle aged woman [it is usually a woman] with a dog or a child, says helpfully "Having trouble? Oh it happened to me; just try your PIN again". So the customer does, but the 'friendly' woman is watching; watching very carefully. She sees what the customer's PIN is, and remembers it, because she is not really being helpful; she is a thief. The customer eventually gives up and goes away. Quickly she takes the thin plastic sheet and the card out of the **ATM** with her nails or tweezers. Now she has your card, and she knows your PIN, so can steal your money, and immediately will.

— if the card goes *over* the plastic, the **ATM** can't tell that there is a card in the slot so when the customer enters the PIN it doesn't work and the same thing happens. Even if the card pops out, the thief has got the PIN, and could make a false card then start to steal your money.

THINK TWICE

If a card sticks in a **cash machine**, stay by it, call your bank from a mobile 'phone, tell them, and they can close the **ATM** from a central point. This stops dishonest people taking your card.

2. Banks

2.7 PIN

**Secret Numbers. What they are. How they work.
How to protect them.**

PIN stands for **Personal Identification Numbers**. This is a series of confidential private numbers that banks give you when you open a bank account. They are 'access codes' to your bank account(s). Banks send your **PIN** through the post. When you get the numbers, memorise them. Don't tell anyone what your numbers are.

Your **PIN** is a secret security number that *only you know.*

You can change your **PIN** to numbers that you can easily remember by following the options given at any ATM cash machine that belongs to your bank. *Don't* choose numbers that are too obvious, such as your birthday or telephone number, because a thief might be able to find them out. If you can't remember your **PIN** you will have to ask your bank for another one.

PINs are used to get money out of your bank account, and to pay for things with a **chip and PIN** card which is a debit or credit card with a computer chip that holds your 4 digit **PIN** number in its memory.

You have to enter your **PIN** into a keypad instead of signing a receipt when you pay for goods and services. The keypad is about the size of a mobile 'phone, and is brought to your table in restaurants and can be found at checkout tills in supermarkets.

If you enter your **PIN** incorrectly 3 times, this will lock your card, so that you cannot use it, and some cash machines will swallow it. If this happens, you have to tell your bank, and ask for a new card. You cannot get  a new card from cash machines. Your bank will send you a new card, and then, separately in a different envelop on a different day, a new **PIN**.

2. Banks

2.8 Debit Card

What they are. How they work.

A **debit card** is a small plastic card which can be used as a method of payment. *Your* money goes out of *your* bank account automatically and instantly.

There are different **debit cards**; some are MAESTRO (formerly SWITCH), VISA DEBIT (DELTA). SOLO is sometimes issued to under 18s.

A **debit card** is not the same as a credit card.

A **debit card** uses ONLY the money that is in the account.

You cannot overdraw on your account with a **debit card** unless you have already arranged an overdraft limit with your bank.

A **debit card** will be sent through the post shortly after you have opened a bank account. When it arrives, sign it immediately with your normal signature.

Most banks offer **debit cards** to customers from age 11 or 12 or older.

When you buy things with a **debit card**, you are instructing your bank to take your money as payment from your account by "electronic fund transfer" at the same time as the card is processed through an electronic machine. So, if you do not have money in your account, **debit cards** will not work, and the shop will tell you that your card has been "refused", and might keep it. This can be embarrassing, so make sure that you have enough money in your account before you use your **debit card**.

A **debit card** can be used for paying for things: on-line with a computer, in shops, restaurants, by telephone, or to get cash back when you buy goods elsewhere. You may be asked to provide the three digit code that is printed at the end of the number on the back of the card, in order to prove that you really do have the card.

Debit cards are used as cheque guarantee cards. See section on cheques overleaf.

There are two ways to use **debit cards** that prove you are who you say you are.

Either: when you use your card you can be asked to sign a piece of paper confirming:

- how much you are paying
- who you are paying it to
- the date

THINK TWICE

Before you sign, make sure the amount is correct.

There are two copies. The shop keeps one, and you keep the other. It is your receipt. Keep it for your end of month budgeting.

Or: you can be asked to enter your own private PIN [Personal Identification Number] on a keypad [Chip and PIN].

THINK TWICE

When you enter your PIN make sure that no-one can see what your number is.

NEVER ask someone else to enter your PIN number.

It is only for you and *nobody else*.

NEVER tell anyone what it is – NOT EVER.

If someone knows your PIN they might be able to rob your bank account, so keep it secret.

You may not get a receipt from the keypad machine, but you should get a receipt from the shop for the things you bought; if you don't, ask for one. Keep it for your end of month account budgeting.

2. Banks

2.9 Cheques

What they are. What they're for.
Potential problems. Definitions.

A **cheque** [spelt "**check**" in North America] is a printed form that is used instead of money to make payments from your bank account.

Cheque guarantee cards are small plastic cards that are used to prove that your bank will pay the money that you write **cheques** for.

Usually they are the same cards as debit cards, and guarantee that your **cheque** will be paid, up to a limit of £100. Write the number on the back of the **cheque**. You may be asked to show this card, if paying by **cheque**.

About cheques

To "post date" a **cheque**
means that you write a future date on it so that it cannot be cashed before that time. This might be because you know that you will not have enough money in your account to cover the amount on the **cheque** till a future date. Tell the person being paid.

To cash a **cheque**
means that you get the money – the cash – by putting the **cheque** into your account.

To stop a **cheque**

[called stop payment on a **check** in North America]
means to prevent your bank from dealing with a **cheque** which you have
written, so that the money is not paid from your bank account. You might
stop a **cheque** if you realise that whatever you paid for with that **cheque**
was broken before you bought it, or it does not exist at all.

To make your **cheques** payable to

someone or a business means to fill in the name of
the person or company that you are paying with the
cheque.

A **banker's draft**

is a **cheque** that has been requested by the person who is being paid
[payee], from bank of the person who is paying [payer], because the
payee thinks that the payer's usual **cheque** might **bounce**. A banker's
draft is a **cheque** that is from the payer's bank itself, instead of directly
from the payer. Money has already been drawn from the payer's account,
and is held by the payer's bank until the payee cashes it. People being
paid think it is more secure. Sometimes this is used as a method of
transferring money internationally between banks in different countries
and between different currencies.

A blank **cheque**

is one that has blank spaces on it. It is incomplete. Although it has been
signed, a blank **cheque** has no amount of money written on it, and
sometimes no name has been written on it either.

THINK TWICE

DO NOT SIGN a **blank cheque**. It is a risky thing to do. It might
be stolen; the thief could then write a large sum of money on it,
then write his/her own name on it, so that the **cheque** seems to
be for them; and the person who signed it – YOU – *would still have
to pay.*

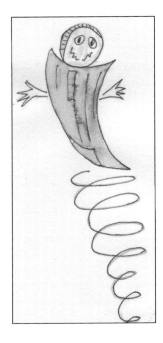

To bounce a **cheque**

is to cause a **cheque** not to be paid.

A bouncing **cheque**

is a **cheque** that is refused [dishonoured] by a bank. The bank bounces it, that is, returns it to the bank account of the writer of the **cheque**. It is bounced back – and the person for whom the **cheque** is written does not get the money. It is usually because there is not

Beee-oing!

enough money in the account, or, might be because a mistake has been made somewhere when the **cheque** was written.

Dishonest people have written **cheques** even though they know that they do not have enough money in their accounts to pay the amount written on the **cheque**. This is why if someone gives you a **cheque**, you must ask for their "cheque guarantee card" [usually a debit card] number and write it on the back of the **cheque** which *guarantees* that any **cheque** up to the value of £100 will be paid.

THINK TWICE

REMEMBER – Many banks still take 3 working days to put **cheques** into bank accounts after they arrive in a bank. For this reason, you have to wait for 3 days before withdrawing that money from your account, but it can take longer to know whether a **cheque** has been bounced [dishonoured], sometimes up to 6 working days.

If your **cheque** bounces, you will have to pay a penalty charge to the bank.

Before electronic transfers became widespread, banks used to say that this 3 day delay allowed them to "clear" **cheques**, so as to be sure that the funds really exist, but, more and more people think that banks deliberately take longer than is now necessary to "clear" **cheques**, because banks benefit by getting 3 days interest from all the many **cheques** that they handle. So, some banks have reduced this time.

2. Banks

2.10 How to Write Cheques

Where to write what. In what order.
How to keep records. Potential problems.

Cheque books are the size of a long thin envelope.

After you have written your **cheques**, they can be torn out of the book along a perforated line.

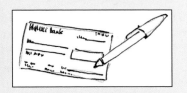

Most cheques look like this:

"Account payee": means this cheque can be paid only into the account of the person/company you write it to: make sure that you ask your bank for "pre-crossed" cheques.

Sort code for your bank

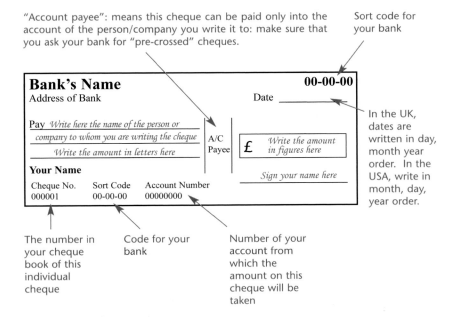

In the UK, dates are written in day, month year order. In the USA, write in month, day, year order.

The number in your cheque book of this individual cheque

Code for your bank

Number of your account from which the amount on this cheque will be taken

Cheque books have a space [stub] either to one side of the **cheques** or on pages at the back or front for recording the details of each **cheque** you write.

Don't forget to do this. Write:

- how much money you wrote the **cheque** for
- to whom or what organisation you wrote the **cheque**
- the date that you wrote the **cheque**
- what the **cheque** is for, maybe you're getting new trainers, cool evening shoes or a DVD.

Keep cheque stubs to compare them with your bank statement each month. Do not throw them away for a year, because you might need them for your tax return, then shred them because they contain private information that thieves could use to rob you of your personal financial identity. Cheque stubs are as valuable to fraudsters as credit cards.

You can ask your bank to print your name on your **cheques** as you want it: Joe Cool; Josie B.Cool; Mr Jo B.Cool; Miss Josephine Cool. The more initials you include the less likely someone will have the same name, thus lowering the chances of being cheated.

When you have written your **cheque** it will look like this:

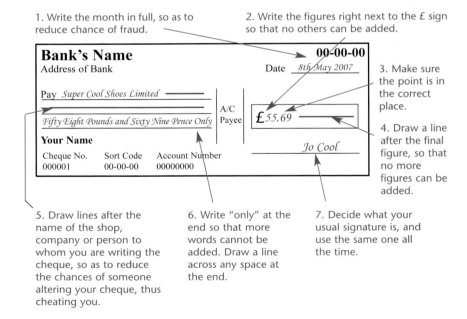

1. Write the month in full, so as to reduce chance of fraud.

2. Write the figures right next to the £ sign so that no others can be added.

3. Make sure the point is in the correct place.

4. Draw a line after the final figure, so that no more figures can be added.

5. Draw lines after the name of the shop, company or person to whom you are writing the cheque, so as to reduce the chances of someone altering your cheque, thus cheating you.

6. Write "only" at the end so that more words cannot be added. Draw a line across any space at the end.

7. Decide what your usual signature is, and use the same one all the time.

Bank's Name
Address of Bank

Date *8th May 2007*

00-00-00

Pay *Super Cool Shoes Limited*

Fifty Eight Pounds and Sixty Nine Pence Only

A/C Payee

£ *55.69*

Your Name

Jo Cool

Cheque No.	Sort Code	Account Number
000001	00-00-00	00000000

CHECK YOUR CHEQUES!

The *last* thing to write on a **cheque** is your signature. It makes it valid.

Take a moment to check that everything is correct and nothing is missing.

You will be asked to show a cheque card, or to write the number of that cheque card on the back of the **cheque**. It guarantees payment of the **cheque** up to a limit, even if you do not have that amount of money in your account. So do not write **cheques** for more money than you have or you will get into debt.

Many banks will not accept **cheques** with mistakes on them. Score out small mistakes so that they are unreadable, then write your initials right next to the correction. The bank should then accept it.

If you make a big mistake, shred or rip up the **cheque** into small pieces destroying the signature and account number, then throw it away.

2. Banks

2.11 Banking Terms – What They Mean

Bank balance. Sort codes. Tellers and cashiers.

> A **bank balance** is the amount of money in a bank account.

A **bank balance** can:

- Have money in it = a positive **balance**, or, be "in the black".
- Be empty – have no money in it. Zero.
- Have minus money in it; be a negative **balance**, be "in the red", in debt, or overdrawn.
- A balance transfer means moving a **balance** from one bank account to another, and it usually refers to moving a debt. Not to paying it back.

> A **sort code**, sometimes called a **sorting code**, is an official number used to refer to a particular bank. It is an identification code for the bank. It consists of a series of 6 numbers that banks use to identify which bank is yours. See 2.9 How to write a cheque.
>
> 01-23-45

You will see these six numbers on your cheques and credit and debit cards.

If you bank over the telephone, you will be asked what your **sort code** is, as part of the verification of your financial identity.

> **Bank teller / Cashier**
>
> People who work in banks, behind the counters, are called **bank tellers**, bank clerks, or **cashiers**. They take your deposits and give you what you withdraw from your account.

2. Banks

2.12 Bank Charges

What to expect. How to find out about them.

> Banks charge for their services.
>
> Different banks have different rates of charges, so find out how much your bank charges for what. Ask for a list giving a breakdown of **bank charges**. Look at the terms and conditions of your bank account. Banks often change what they charge for, and the amount they charge, so read all letters from your bank carefully.

Here are some general examples of the things banks charge for:

— Transferring money to accounts in other banks.
— Payments into and out of your account(s), though not all banks do this.
— Standing orders and Direct debits.
— Interest on loans and overdrafts; the rates will be agreed in advance. If you do not know the rate of interest, DO NOT sign the agreement.
— Fees for arranging and managing loans and overdrafts.
— Bouncing cheques.
— Issuing bankers' drafts.
— Any amount not paid on a credit card bill, even if the minimum required is paid.
— Withdrawing your money out of other banks' ATMs.
— Withdrawing your money out of ATMs abroad.
— Travellers' cheques.
— Converting currencies on withdrawals from ATMs abroad.

 See section on Exchange Rate

— Getting overdrawn on any amount: even if you have an agreed overdraft limit, you will be charged; and, if you spend over that limit, that is, spend the bank's money, you will be charged more.

If a Direct Debit or Standing Order has automatically been paid, thus putting your account in debt (making you overdrawn), then banks will charge a set maintenance charge per month for paying them, PLUS a fee per Direct Debit or Standing Order, PLUS interest on the amount by which you are overdrawn.

If there is not enough money in the account, then banks will not pay any more Direct Debits or Standing Orders, but they will charge a "referral fee" for refusing to pay them, PLUS interest on the amount by which you are overdrawn.

AS WELL AS THIS the companies with which you have agreed to pay Direct Debits and Standing Orders will either stop giving you the service that you are paying for, and/or, demand a late payment fee, and after a month or two may collect the debt using Debt Collectors.

2. Banks

2.13 Bank Statement

What they are. What information they give. How to decipher them. Description and example.

> A **bank statement** is a printed paper record of the money that goes in and is taken out of a bank account.

At the end of each month, or every quarter of each year, whichever you ask for, your bank will send you a statement, by post to your address.

Bank statements contain important information. They show:

- the date on which money is paid in or withdrawn from your account. This is sometimes a day or two after the date of the transaction, except with debit card transactions which are debited from your account immediately.
- how much you have paid to whom, but not for what.
- how much the bank has charged you for their services.

To find out how much your bank charges for overdrafts and other services, look in the bank's leaflets' small-print, or simply ask.

THINK TWICE

BEWARE – Check on your **statement** that all the cheques are ones that you really have written, and that they are for the correct amount of money.

Check that each withdrawal and deposit you know about is written on your statement.

REMEMBER – If you overspend, your account will be overdrawn. You have spent the bank's money, and you owe them a debt.

Some banks use the letters "DR" in the balance column meaning overdrawn. Some banks use a minus [-] to show overdrawn amounts. Some banks write overdrawn figures in red, so you have to look closely.

Bank charges

Most banks charge for any amount of overdraft, agreed or not. All banks charge for any amount that you spend beyond your agreed overdraft limit, because you have overspent and will be in debt, therefore the bank *will charge*.

These are some of the likely kinds of bank charges:

1. a flat fee in any month that your account is overdrawn: usually about £28/ £42 that is removed from your account 16 days after the date that your **statement** is issued.

2. either:

   a "card misuse charge" for each transaction you make that the bank has been forced to pay (honour), because you have used either a cheque guarantee card or a debit card and thus you have spent money that *you do not have*. In other words, you have spent the bank's money, NOT your own money, so you owe the bank a debt. Usually the charge is about £25 / £40 per item.

   or:

   a "returned unpaid charge" which means that the bank has had to return a direct debit, standing order or cheque (used without a cheque guarantee card) because you do not have enough money in your account. Usually the charge is about £25 / £40 per item.

3. a "paid referral charge" if your account is overdrawn more than about £25 / £35 beyond your agreed limit. Some banks charge this *per day* that you are overdrawn.

4. interest on the overdrawn amount, *on top of the other charges*. The amount of interest varies according to the kind of account you have, which is partly dependant on your credit history.

THINK TWICE

REMEMBER – Sometimes transactions shown on bank statements are dated a day or two later than when they really happen.

Every month look through your statement. See End of Month Reckoning/ Budgeting.

Knowledge is power. Make sure you KNOW what is happening to your MONEY.

Look at the bank statement on the following pages. You will see:

DD meaning Direct Debit followed by the words "miraculous mobiles"; this person has arranged a direct debit with a mobile 'phone company: "Miraculous Mobiles".

Debit card for shopping at Tedious Supermarkets, plus cash back of £50.00.

ATM [cash machine] showing where and how much was withdrawn: £100.00

Then the bank has paid interest into the account. This means that the account must have been in credit, not overdrawn.

On 12th May a cheque for £50 was paid in. Several other payments have been made with a debit card, then another withdrawal from an ATM.

Next is a standing order to an insurance company for £40. It puts the account into debt. This person has spent the bank's money. From this point BEWARE...!

The account is overdrawn [DR] This is shown by a minus [-] on 20th May in front of the figure £-23.10 Sometimes negative amounts are printed in red.

As the arranged overdraft limit is £100 [see the top of the statement] there is no overdraft charge – YET. On 23 May cash back from Dreary Supermarket pushed the overdraft above the agreed limit, so from this point the account is overdrawn beyond the agreed amount and therefore will be *charged interest*. **TROUBLE..!**

Banks charge interest *immediately*. Also, a flat fee is charged once in any month on any amount overdrawn. Here, it's for £28.

Then, a cheque was written and a cheque guarantee card must have been used because the bank has paid this cheque (honoured it) and this has put the account even deeper in debt. Therefore £35 has been charged, and this amount will be charged on *each transaction* after the account is in debt beyond the agreed overdraft limit.

On 30 May there is a direct credit payment of a monthly salary, but it is too late to stop the bank charges for this month, because the account was overdrawn beyond the agreed limit.

As soon as the salary is paid-in, spending starts again; a monthly bus pass is bought.

The total figures refer to payments and total receipts, then the balance is shown.

The balance is the amount remaining in your account. It is the figure on the bottom right of the statement. In this case the balance is £1,883.73

The owner of this account has not budgeted wisely. If a little less had been spent, there would have been no bank charges. The account holder bought clothes as well as an expensive bicycle. S/he must have known that a standing order would be paid at the end of the month, so should have cut back on spending just enough not to get overdrawn beyond the agreed limit. The bank charges on this overdraft were removed automatically by the bank.

This person had to pay bank charges of a £28 flat fee for being overdrawn in any month, + £35 for each transaction over the overdraft limit = £35x2=70, + debtor interest on the amount overdrawn beyond the agreed limit @3% of £172.77 = £5.18, which is a total of £102.28 in bank charges.

This person did not pay attention to what they were doing with their own money.

It's almost like giving a present of £102.28 to the bank!

A bank statement looks something like this:

Roll number is number of the roll of the special banking paper that your statement is printed on. It is for bank reference only.

BIC is the swift code. IBAN is the international banking code.

Overdrafts must be arranged in advance with your bank.

Make sure that the Balance Brought Forward is the same figure as the balance at the end of last month's **bank statement**.

Date					
Bank's Bar Code	Statement number 01		Name & Address of Bank		
Your Name & Address			Roll Number: A/000000-0		
			Sort Code: 00-00-00		
BANK ACCOUNT STATEMENT			Account Number: 00000000		
Your arranged overdraft limit is £100			BIC ABCD EFG 0H		
			IBAN AB12 CDE 3456 789012		
			Page 1 of 1		

Note the minus. It means that this account is in debt. This is a negative amount.

Some banks write "DR" to show that the account is overdrawn. Others write "minus", or use the symbol "-", and some use red ink.

Date	Description	Payments	Receipts	Balance
	Balance brought forward			983.34
3 May 07	DD: Miraculous Mobiles	19.48		963.86
5 May 07	Debit card - Tedious S/Mkt Anytown	37.74		944.41
9 May 07	Debit card cash back - Tedious S/Mkt	50.00		906.67
9 May 07	ATM Tawdry Street, Plainton	100.00		856.67
11 May 07	Interest Credited		2.10	756.67
12 May 07	Cheque 0000 00 00 00		50.00	725.47
15 May 07	Debit Card - Tardy Rail Travel Ltd	45.59		652.47
16 May 07	Debit Card - Cool Clothes Inc	159.99		606.88
	Debit Card - Fab Bike Company	329.99		446.89
	Debit Card - Nice Bistro Cafe	23.89		116.90
	ATM Dull Street, London	100.00		16.90
20 May 07	SO Somewhat Safe Insurance Co.	40.00		-23.10DR
23 Mat 07	Debit Card - Dreary S/Mkt, Anytown	101.67		-74.77DR
	Charges	28.00		-152.77DR
23 May 07	Cheque 0000 00 00 01	20.00		-172.77DR
24 May 07	Charges	70.00		-242.77DR
24 May 07	Interest	5.18		-247.95DR
30 May 07	Direct Credit - Mediocre Employers		2,150.99	1,903.04
31 May 07	Uncomfy Bus Company	59.49		1,843.55
	Total	1,191.02	2,203.09	£1,843.55

Charges start as soon as the account is overdrawn. Flat fee charged once in any month that the account is overdrawn beyond the agreed limit.

The account gets out of debt here. This is a positive amount.

Security advice - To safeguard your account never give anyone your personal security details, including passwords, security numbers or PINs. If you loose your card or cheque book, or they are stolen call us 24 hours a day on 00000 00 00 00.

To help avoid charges on your bank account, you should ensure sufficient funds are in your account to pay Standing Orders and Direct Debits, the day before payment is due. The payment and charge decision is made at the time of the transaction, and not based on the balance at the end of that day.

Bank's registration and regulatory information.

SO stands for Standing Order.

A flat fee is charged for *each transaction* after the account is overdrawn beyond the agreed limit.

This person had to pay bank charges of a £28 flat fee for being overdrawn in any month, + £35 for each transaction over the overdraft limit = £35x2=70, + debtor interest on the amount overdrawn beyond the agreed limit @3% of £172.77 = £5.18, which is a total of £102.28 in bank charges. This person did not pay attention to what they were doing with their own money. It's almost like giving a present of £102.28 to the bank!

2. Banks

2.14 Cash Back

What. Where. How.

> This is another way of using your debit or credit card to withdraw money from your bank account.

In many countries in large supermarkets it is possible to withdraw money from your bank account at the same time as paying for goods. This is called **cash back**.

Large shops such as supermarkets require you to spend a minimum amount, which they decide on, before you can ask the person at the till for cash back. Usually there is an upper limit of **cash back** of about £50. The amount depends on the shop's policy.

Make sure that the amount you withdraw in this way is shown on your receipt from the shop.

Banks

2.15 Deposit

What is it. How to do it. Potential for confusion.

> To **deposit** money is to pay money into a bank account.
>
> A **safe deposit box**, or **safety deposit box** is a strong box in a bank where you can keep money or other valuable things.

If money is **on deposit** it means that money is saved in a bank or other financial institution.

To **deposit** money into any bank account, including your own, you can take cash to a bank, send or take a cheque to a bank, or arrange that you are paid by someone else using direct credit or standing order into your bank account. You need to know the number of the bank account, the address of the bank and the bank sort code.

When sending a cheque to your bank, either use one of the bank's **deposit** slips or, write a short note like this:

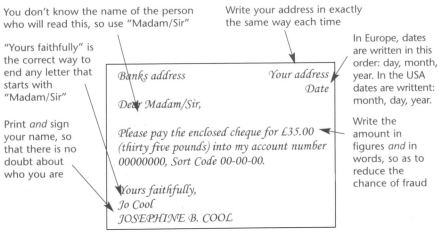

You don't know the name of the person who will read this, so use "Madam/Sir"

Write your address in exactly the same way each time

"Yours faithfully" is the correct way to end any letter that starts with "Madam/Sir"

Print *and* sign your name, so that there is no doubt about who you are

In Europe, dates are written in this order: day, month, year. In the USA dates are writtent: month, day, year.

Write the amount in figures *and* in words, so as to reduce the chance of fraud

Banks address

Your address

Date

Dear Madam/Sir,

Please pay the enclosed cheque for £35.00 (thirty five pounds) into my account number 00000000, Sort Code 00-00-00.

Yours faithfully,
Jo Cool
JOSEPHINE B. COOL

Most banks provide "quick pay-in envelopes" for notes of up to about £250, on which there is space to write the account holder's name, sort code, account number, post code, date and amount of money enclosed. Seal envelope and place in box inside bank.

The short letter gives all the information the bank needs; no more, and no less: your full name, your account number, sort code, your address and the date. It is not necessary to say who the cheque is from. Remember to put the cheque in the envelope.

It is important to keep a record of cheques that you have sent to your bank, so that you know what is correct when you see your bank statement, and for use when doing your end of month reckoning.

Keep a note of how much you **deposit** in which account. You will need this record for your end of month reckoning.

If you go to a bank, the bank teller will give you a receipt. If you send a cheque to your bank, you will not get a receipt but the amount on the cheque will be written on your bank statement showing when and how much was **paid-in**.

Some ATMs allow money to be **deposited** through a slot. See section 2.6 ATMs.

Another way of **depositing** money is to put it into a **night safe**, which is a small hatch in the wall of a bank, outside in the street.

Night safes are used by small businesses that make lots of cash. Banks give these customers a key to the **night safe**, and small lockable and labelled wallets for the cash. After the banks are closed, these special wallets can be put it through the little hatch that leads to the bank's **night safe**. Later, the **night safe** is opened by bank staff and the money is taken out of the wallets and **deposited** into the customers' bank accounts. It is a way of making sure that the cash that people have earned is safe overnight. Banks charge their customers for this **deposit** arrangement.

THINK TWICE

Deposit also has another meaning:

it can mean a sum of money which is given in advance as part of a total payment for something. You can leave a **deposit** so that shop assistants will keep a dress for you till the next day.

OR

a sum of money which you pay when you rent something, and which is returned to you when you return the thing you have rented, in good condition.

50

2. Banks

2.16 Withdrawal

What it is. Ways to do it. Potential problems.

> **Withdrawing money** means to to take money out of a bank account.

There are several ways to **withdraw** money from your bank account:

In a bank. If you go into a bank to make a **withdrawal** from your account, you have to fill-in a "**withdrawal** slip" which you give to a bank teller who then gives you your money. You will be given a receipt too. Keep the receipt and use it for your end of month account check.

From a cash machine [ATM] using a debit card, and a PIN. Keep notes of how much you **withdraw**, Put any little financial notes to yourself in a folder and keep them for your end of month reckoning. If you use ATMs belonging to your own bank there is usually no charge for this service, for now, though some banks may change this in the future.

Using cash back services in a supermarket using your debit or credit card. Keep the receipt. There is no charge either from the bank or from the supermarket. This is a cheap a way of **withdrawing** money.

With a direct debit or standing order arrangement with your bank. Check this at the end of each month by looking at your bank statement. Banks charge for these services.

By writing a cheque to yourself. You can get money immediately with this method, but the amount of money you **withdraw** from your account will not show on your statement for 3 working days because that is how long it takes banks to process cheques – for now, though this may speed up soon. Write on the cheque book stub how much each cheque is for.

By bank transfer. You can ask your bank to move money from one account to another, or from one bank to another. If you move money from one account to another within the same bank sometimes there is no charge, but if you transfer money to another account in a different bank, whether or not it is yours, there will be a fee. The amount is **withdrawn** from your account, and moved to the place you want it to be. There are usually 3 speeds available at graded costs. The fastest is done on the same day that you request it, the next takes 2 business days, and the slowest takes 5 business days to complete.

THINK TWICE

But – BEWARE

From a cash machine [ATM] using a credit card and a PIN.

Although you get money immediately, this method is *NOT a real* **withdrawal** from a bank account.

Instead it is *borrowing money* from a credit card company that is associated with your bank. Even if you pay back this money as soon as you get the credit card bill, you will still be paying a percentage for the privilage of borrowing money in this way.

It is one of the MOST EXPENSIVE ways to borrow money, so, should be used rarely. Keep it in mind for emergency **withdrawals** only.

2. Banks

2.17 Direct credit

What it is. How it works.

> **Direct credit** [called **direct deposit** in North America], is an arrangement in which money is moved electronically into a bank account.

Your hard-earned money

Direct credit is the method that many employers use to pay salaries directly into employees' bank accounts.

It is more secure than paying people by handing them envelopes of cash, or by sending them cheques, either of which could be more easily stolen.

It works using the electronic transfer system of BACS Payment Scheme.

Each employee tells the employer their bank account number and sort code. This information tells the employer where to send the salary. The salary is then paid into the account on the same date each month. In this way employees always know exactly when the money that they have earned will be in their bank accounts.

DIRECT CREDIT IS A WAY OF GETTING PAID

2. Banks

2.18 Central Bank

What they are. What they are for.

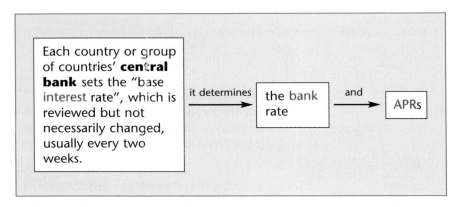

Each country or group of countries' **central bank** sets the "base interest rate", which is reviewed but not necessarily changed, usually every two weeks.

it determines → the bank rate → and → APRs

In most countries **Central Banks** are government owned. They are the main monetary authority that is responsible for the stability of the national currency. They issue money, regulate the supply of credit, supervise banking activities, hold the "reserves" of other banks and can store other countries' money.

Bank reserves are the part of capital/principal that is not invested, or, a portion of profits that are not distributed by a bank or business.

Central Banks put into practice the monetary policies of their governments.

A **Central Bank** is a government monetary authority that issues currency and regulates the supply of credit.

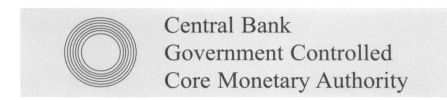

Central Bank
Government Controlled
Core Monetary Authority

3. Borrowing Money

3.1 Borrowing Money

What borrowing involves. Pros & cons. Who from. How to handle it. What happens.

> ### Not as simple as it first appears...

> To **borrow** is to take an agreed amount of money from someone or from a financial institution and pay it back over a period of time. You owe the money.
>
> To **lend** is to give money to someone who agrees that they will pay it back in the future, usually with additional money added to the original amount. Banks and other organizations lend money.
>
> A **lender** is the person or financial institution that lends money.

If you **borrow** money, it's NOT REALLY YOURS until you have paid it all back. You owe it to someone. The money you have **borrowed** really belongs to the **lender**, and **lenders** make you pay extra for having their money until you pay it back. The extra is "interest".

Borrowers pay back the amount **borrowed**, called "capital sum", or "principal sum", PLUS the interest as well. You can agree with the **lender** to pay it back all in one go at a certain date, or you can agree to pay it back bit by bit, usually each month.

? TO BORROW, OR NOT TO BORROW ?

Advantages of borrowing money:

- You can get it quickly. You can use it to buy what you want immediately.
- You might buy something that you will use every day, or that, over a long time, can be used to help save money – such as a bicycle, so you stop paying bus fares.

Disadvantages of borrowing money:

- You have to pay it all back. You owe it to someone.
- You have to pay the agreed amount back at the agreed time.
- You have to pay back more than the amount you borrow, just for the privilege of borrowing it. The extra amount is the interest on the loan.
- If you cannot pay back the amount you have **borrowed**, at the correct time, you loose the interest you have paid, plus, if you have borrowed from a shop to buy something, you will lose what you bought with the **borrowed** money, because the **lender** still owns it. This would be very upsetting.

BEFORE BORROWING MONEY, ASK YOURSELF: IF I BORROW THIS MONEY, WILL I *REALLY* BE ABLE TO PAY IT BACK?

THINK TWICE

BEWARE – Do not consider **borrowing**, unless from a reputable bank or building society. Just because a bank offers to lend money to you, does not necessarily mean that they think you can pay it back. As soon as people get into debt, banks can charge interest, and that is one of the ways that banks make money. If you do not pay back the agreed amount of money in the agreed time, you are called a debtor or defaulter.

If you are in default, the **lender** has the right to collect all of the money that you have **borrowed**. The **lender** can do this even if you do not have the money, by taking away things [collateral] from your house which have the same value as the amount of money you owe. See section 6.5 about debt collecting agencies.

The best way to stop this happening is NEVER to default on paying back a debt.

NEVER STOP PAYING BACK A DEBT UNTIL IT IS ALL PAID OFF...

You cannot hide it if you stop paying back a debt. Your name will be on a national debt collecting agency list, on computer. Banks keep these lists and know if you have ever stopped paying back a debt.

You will be given a "bad credit rating", or "poor credit score" which can be serious, because in the future if you want to borrow money to buy a car, or a house with a mortgage, it might be difficult for you to do so, because the lenders will think that you are the kind of person who does not pay back debts, so they will charge you a higher rate of interest, or, may not want to lend to you at all.

Debt can grow out of control very quickly. See section 6.1 on debt.

3. Borrowing Money

3.2 Interest

What it is. How you get it. How you pay it. Different kinds. How it is calculated. Examples. Potential problems.

Interest, in money terms, is nothing to do with anything being... interesting.

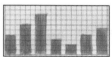

> **Interest** is additional or "extra" money, calculated as a percentage [%]
>
> It's a supplement, or, "extra" that is paid to you if you save your money in a bank.
>
> and
>
>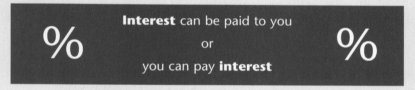
>
> it's the extended add-on amount, or, "extra" that you pay if you borrow money.
>
> **Interest rates** are the levels at which financial institutions (banks, building societies and loan companies) set percentages [%] for the "extra" money.

Different banks charge different **interest rates** for various services.

Interest rates change according to government policy, political and financial situations around the world, and are announced in newspapers and other media.

The **interest rate** that you pay a bank is usually slightly higher than the **interest** rate that a bank pays you. It's partly how banks make money.

The **bank rate** [official discount rate] is the rate of **interest** at which banks lend to commercial banks and other financial institutions. It is the amount of **interest** that banks charge, particularly the lowest amount that they are allowed to charge, when they lend money.

Interest rates can and often do change. Banks' **interest** rates are announced each week in the press. Look in the money pages of good quality newspapers or on the internet.

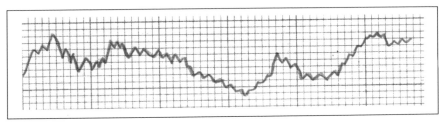

Look carefully.
There are many different interest rates

Interest rates for borrowing vary depending on your credit score, employment status, age and your other financial commitments. They vary from about 4.50% to about 6.00% or as much as 7.00%, or even higher, if the lender considers you a high risk.

EXCEPT...

BEWARE – see section on Borrowing, especially shop cards and credit cards!

Interest can be paid:

- each month = *monthly*, or per month.
- each quarter of a year = *quarterly*, or per quarter.
- each year = *annually*, or per annum.

according to the Financial Year.

Interest that you pay

THINK TWICE

If you borrow money, remember that it is NOT REALLY YOURS UNTIL YOU HAVE PAID IT ALL BACK.

You have to pay **interest** on the money you borrow. When you pay **interest**, it means that you pay what you owe, PLUS "extra" which is the **interest**.

When you sign an agreement to borrow money, you agree to pay **interest** on the amount you borrow.

How much **interest** you agree to pay, depends on from where you borrow and your credit score.

If you get into debt, you have to pay **interest** on the money you owe.

Example

If you have borrowed £1,000 at 5% **interest** (per year), you must repay £1,000 plus 5% of £1,000 = £50, which comes to a total debt of £1,050.

If the **interest** must be paid per month, then you will have to pay a monthly sum which will include part of the £1,000 you borrowed and some interest. For example, if you paid back £1,000 over 12 months, you might have to pay monthly interest on £1,000 (£50 ÷ 12 months = £4.16 per month). So, if you have agreed to pay back £100 of the debt itself per month, plus the £4.16 of **interest**, then, each month you will have to pay back £104.16. Thus, if, and only if, you continue to pay this amount each month, on time, for 10 months, then soon after the end of month 10, and by month 11, you will have paid back your whole debt.

Interest you are paid

If your account is in credit, you are paid **interest**. If you have chosen to put your money in an **interest** bearing bank account, sometimes called savings account, then you will be paid a percentage [%] on the amount of money that you have.

For example if you have £10,000 in a savings account on which the **interest rate** is 4%, you will be paid 4% of 10,000 (which is £400). So, at the end of the year you will have £10,400. You can do whatever you want with that 4%. Either leave it in the bank for another year, ask the bank to send it to another bank or building society, or take it out of your bank account and spend it.

What would you spend an extra £400 on?

BEWARE – Some **interest** payments have rules (conditions) attached to them, such as penalty payments if you choose to withdraw your money earlier than you first agreed.

Some religions have rules about interest.
To find out consult a religious official.

Different kinds of interest

Simple interest is **interest** paid on the principal (capital) alone.

Compound Interest is **interest** calculated on both the principal (capital) and the accumulated (accrued) **interest**. When the **interest** that is earned on an investment is put back into the account where it came from, it is added to the "principal" amount and all future **interest** from then on, is calculated on the new, larger, "principal". So, if you are saving money, you are in effect getting **interest** on the **interest**.

Note that certain religious people of some faiths do not encourage the use of interest. To find out, ask someone knowledgeable about this aspect of belief.

See section 3.4 on APR [Annual Percentage Rate].

See section 6.1 on debt.

Albert Einstein said that

Compound Interest is
"the greatest mathematical discovery of the world"
and he called it
"the ninth wonder of the world."

3. Borrowing Money

3.3 Price Variations

**Why prices change. How these changes are measured.
Inflation & deflation. What they are. When they
happen. Cost of living. What it is.
Price index. What it is.**

Inflation

Inflation is the rate of increase of prices. In moderation, it is regarded as healthy for the economy of countries.

Prices increase at various rates because of expansion in demand for goods, or an increase in the money supply.

Going Up

Deflation is the rate of decrease in prices. In moderation it is regarded as a set back. It can happen during an economic recession when there is a reduction in the amount of money in circulation. **Deflation** can cause a crisis; though prices may be cheaper, people cannot afford to buy much. Extreme **deflation** is usually bad for production and employment.

Hyperinflation is an extremely high rate of inflation, which makes a country's currency worth very little or nothing.

A **sub-prime** is a loan that is high risk. "Sub" means below, and "prime" refers to something at its best, meaning that in terms of money that can be made by lenders, such loans are less than top quality. **Sub-prime** loans are usually mortgages recklessly lent to people who, realistically, will never be able to pay them back. Both borrowers and lenders of these loans tend to be regarded as irresponsible. If financial institutions subsequently sell and resell such loans between each other it is likely to contribute to a credit crunch which can affect global financial situations.

A **credit crunch** is a time span during which there is a sudden reduction in availability of loans, both personal and business, from and between banks. It can happen during economic downturns or recessions. A credit squeeze is a less fearful way of describing the same thing.

Liquidity is the easy ability with which assets such as houses can be turned into money. Lack of liquidity can occur during a credit crunch.

Negative growth is shrinkage or reduction of a country's economic growth over a time span of two consecutive quarters of a financial year.

Cost of living

The Cost of living refers to the average cost of basic necessities of life such as food, shelter and clothing.

It is calculated on the average shopping basket of certain ordinary items.

A rise in the **cost of living** would make the rate of **inflation** rise.

Price index

Price indexes measure the change in the **cost of living**. They are used to compare prices over a set time, and to compare prices in different places.

Changes in interest rate

Governments or central banks change interest rates – you will hear monthly about decisions being made about keeping them the same, or changing them. They do this to manage inflation and keep the cost of living down. The effect is important because it affects the cost of money to you on bank accounts, credit cards and other things. It also changes the rewards for saving if interest rates change.

3. Borrowing Money

3.4 Annualised Percentage Rate [APR]

APR & Bank rate. What they are. How they work. Potential for confusion. Example.

APR stands for the **annualised percentage rate [APR]**. It is the compounded amount of interest over a

year that different financial institutions – banks, building societies, store cards, credit and debit cards – charge their customers for lending them money.

> ### THINK TWICE
>
> Compare the APRs that different financial institutions offer.

The **APR** [percentage rate of interest, compounded over a year] is not necessarily the same as any quoted interest rate, because, interest rates can be given as monthly interest rates or as yearly (annual) interest rates.

If financial institutions offer a "fixed **APR**", it means that the **APR** does not change for a set length of time. Ask for *how* long.

If the **APR** is "variable", it means that the **APR** changes whenever the financial institutions change the amount of interest that they charge. They do this depending on government interest rates and other global political and financial situations, which can be effected by climate, wars, international treaties, trade, important countries' economies and many other things.

%%%%%%

THINK TWICE

BEWARE – It is easy to confuse monthly **interest rates** with **APRs** = percentage rate of interest, compounded *over a year*.

APRs are not the same as AERs.

When you are comparing interest rates offered by different banks or different bank accounts.

Compare:

APRs with **APRs** – *annual* (yearly) rates with other *annual* rates

and

monthly interest rates with *monthly* interest rates.

DO NOT compare monthly interest rates with **APRs**. They are different things.

Sometimes **APRs** do not include fees for administration of a loan.

When assessing banks, bank accounts, and most particularly if you are considering using the very expensive store credit cards, find out how much their **APR** is, and what other fees are included – so that you can compare costs properly.

APRs can be calculated using compound interest. Banks & financial institutions charge monthly interest. Over a year the interest charged compounds.

If you borrow £100 at the interest rate of 1% a month, then the interest rate is 12% a year, BUT the **APR** is 12.68% because you get charged interest on the interest. So

- at the end of January you would be charged 1%; by then you would owe £101.00
- if you have not paid off January's payment, at the end of February you would be charged 1% on £101.00. As 1% of £101 = £1.01 - then you would owe £102.01.
- at the end of March £102.01 plus 1% = £1.02; then you would owe £103.03. And so on: at the end of December you would owe £112.68.

The higher the rate of interest, the larger is the compound effect.

3. Borrowing Money

3.5 AER – Annual Equivalent Rate
EIR – Effective Interest Rate

Explains this interest rate

AER is *not* the same as APR.

A.E.R. stands for "Annual Equivalent Rate" of interest. **AER** is used when interest is charged or paid more frequently than once each year. It indicates what the rate of interest would be, if interest was paid or charged just once a year.

REMEMBER – Interest can be money that you pay, or, money that you are paid. See section 3.2 Interest.

It is the yearly [annual] equivalent rate of a daily or monthly interest rate.

Usually it is the interest rate that is charged on arranged [agreed] overdrafts.

You will see **AER** written after percentages on applications for overdrafts.

The interest rate for arranged overdrafts is usually shown on overdraft applications as a daily percentage, followed by a bracketed figure. Usually it is written like this:

"0.71% per month (8.9% AER)"

The first figure is the daily interest rate. The second figure is the annual equivalent interest rate: **AER**. It is the yearly [annual] equivalent of the interest that your bank offers per day or per month for any particular service.

The **Annual Equivalent Rate [AER]** is quoted in loan advertisements so that it is easier to compare financial products that banks and other financial institutions try to sell you. **AER** is the corresponding yearly interest rate of the interest rate for *each day* or *month*. It is NOT the **APR**, because it is not charged/ paid per year [annually].

The interest rate that you are charged for agreed overdrafts, is charged per day, NOT monthly or yearly, but can be expressed *as though it were* an Annual Percentage Rate APR. It is referred to as an **AER** or sometimes a yearly rate. Although it is charged daily, and is removed monthly, it is still called an Annual rate.

THINK TWICE

BEWARE – Do not confuse **AER** with APR.

Most banks usually charge about 9% for the service of an agreed overdraft.

Find out how much **AER** your bank charges.

Remember - this charge is dependant on how much you are overdrawn because it is a percentage.

£%€%$%£

3. Borrowing Money

3.6 Loan and Lender

**How loans work. Different kinds & rates.
Who offers them. What they cost**

A **loan**, sometimes called **credit**, **an advance**, or **finance**, is a sum of money borrowed by one individual or organization from another. A **loan** has to be paid back, usually with interest.

Having a **loan** is a debt.

A **money lender** sometimes just called a **lender** is someone or something that lends money, especially a large financial organization such as a bank.

A **"secured loan"** is a **loan** that is made safer for the **lender** by identifying some of the borrower's possessions, and agreeing that, if the borrower does not pay back the **loan**, or is late paying it, the **lender** can take away and keep these things. In **loan** agreements these possessions are called *"collateral"*. Collateral can sometimes be electronic goods such as TVs, DVD players, fridges, washing-machines, a car or even a house. If you do not pay your **loan** debts, these things will belong to the **lender**.

Unsecured loans do not have any possessions identified as "security", so are more expensive, that is, the interest rate is higher, than for s**ecured loans**.

Loan rates are the amount of interest charged for borrowing money.

Legitimate **loan**, finance or credit companies are employed by shops to arrange and manage interest free and interest bearing purchases, BUT beware of **loan sharks** [loan companies, or 'door-step lenders'].

A **loan shark** is a person or company that charges VERY LARGE amounts of interest for lending money to someone.

They are money **lenders** who are sometimes dishonest, and may also be illegal. They will lend money when nobody else will. They may try to cheat people by asking them to pay a fee before they get the **loan**, then refuse to give the **loan** and keep the fee!

People they try to lend to are usually poor so they have little chance of being able to pay off the **loans**. They charge HUGELY HIGH interest rates; have complicated contracts and severe penalties for default. They can be rough and very nasty and have been known to use physical force to take possessions from people who cannot repay their loans.

AVOID THEM.

They are called "sharks" for a good reason – they'll eat you up given half the chance!

Borrowing Money

3.7 Credit Score

What it is. Why it is important. How it is used.

A **credit score** is part of each person's Financial Identity.

As soon as you open a bank account you start to build up your own personal **credit score**.

Also referred to as:
**credit record / rating / history,
financial record / rating / history.**

A **credit score** is unique personal information about your finances that records any default on borrowing that you have had in the past.

A **credit score** is an evaluation of your financial life.

From it, calculations can be made about your ability to pay back money that you have borrowed, or plan to borrow. These calculations are called **credit referencing**. Organisations called credit referencing agencies carry out investigative checks on behalf of potential lenders, so that they can find out about your financial behaviour.

Reliable?
Dependable?
Honest?
Cost-conscious?

OR

Irresponsible?
Spendthrift?
Shop-aholic?
Wasteful?

If you want to borrow money, potential lenders can look up your **credit rating** to find out whether you are a reliable person to lend money to.

If you have not paid a debt, such as a utility bill [electricity, gas, water or telephone] this will be on your personal **financial record**.

A **credit history** tells potential lenders whether you are likely to pay back any money that you might try to borrow. To have **bad credit**, or to be a **bad credit risk** means that someone has an unstable **credit history**.

Which Are You?

OUT OF CONTROL	IN CONTROL
Debtor	Economic
Defaulter	Prudent
Profligate	Thrifty
Extravagant	Frugal
Can't organise own spending	Manages own money

THINK TWICE

REMEMBER – Lenders want to make money. They are unlikely to choose to lend if they think that they will never be able to get their money back (recover the debt). They prefer to lend to people who will pay their debts – with interest.

> If you do not pay your debts,
> it may be on your **financial record** for ever.

All of your financial life is dependent on having a good **credit history**. It is part of your own personal financial identity.

Without a good **financial record** you may never be allowed to get credit cards, loans or even mortgages to buy a house in the future.

3. Borrowing Money

3.8 Instalment Plans / Hire Purchase

How they work. What they cost.

Instalment Payment Plans, **Hire Purchase** and **Interest Free Credit** agreements are similar but not quite the same.

All of these methods of paying are MORE EXPENSIVE than paying the whole cost of something immediately. You have to pay *more frequently* and a *larger total amount* than you would if you were to pay the whole cost straight away, AND you owe someone money while you are paying the instalments.

> **Hire purchase** is a method of paying for things by paying part of the cost immediately and the rest in smaller regular payments until the debt is completely paid. It is a system of credit, which is a kind of debt.
>
> **Hire purchase** is sometimes called "buying on the never-never" meaning that people *feel* that the payments never end.

If something costs £350, say, a bicycle; there are four ways of paying for it:

1. paying the whole amount immediately, either with cash, a cheque or with a debit card. You own it. The bike is yours. That is that.

2. paying the whole amount immediately with a credit card which is borrowing money from your bank. You owe your bank the cost of the bike, and have to pay it back when you get the credit card bill.

3. paying by **hire purchase** which means that, in effect, you hire something while you are buying it. You pay a part of the cost each month [monthly instalments], usually by direct debit, or standing order. During those months, although you ride the bicycle and keep it in your house, it is NOT YET YOURS. Legally, it belongs to the **hire purchase** company, AND if you do not continue to pay for it each month, they have the right, on behalf of the shop, to come to your house and take

it away. The cost of any repairs or alterations that happened, after you bought the bike, are new costs separate from, and *in addition to* the cost of buying the bicycle.

4. paying with an **instalment plan**, advertised as **credit available** or **easy terms**, which means that you take out a loan from either the seller's bank or your own bank. This is borrowing money. Usually it is repaid with direct debits.

> Pay more, over months and months and months

The way it works is that you agree to pay a certain amount of money to the seller each month. You sign a mandate – a bank document – to set up a direct debit. The seller has an agreement with their bank and you sign an agreement with the seller allowing them to collect direct debts from your bank.

THINK TWICE

If you do not have enough money in your bank account to pay the direct debit, then the seller will get in contact with you and ask you to pay the money that you owe. Usually this will happen twice, then, if you still cannot pay, your OWN bank will cancel the direct debit instruction. This would be very bad because not only do you still owe money to the seller but you also now owe money to your own bank, because banks charge for having to cancel direct debits that are not paid.

BEWARE – In this way, you get deeper in debt.

THINK TWICE

If you still do not have enough money in your bank account to pay your debt, then the seller will employ a debt collector to take things from your house of the equivalent value.

BEWARE – This is very serious, and can be extremely upsetting.

REMEMBER – All debts will be on your credit history.

The law in some places, such as in Scotland, allows the seller to go through the law courts and serve "an arrestment" on your bank account which allows them to remove the sum of money that you owe them from your bank account. Not only this, but *in addition* YOUR bank will ALSO remove the same amount of money from your bank account. Your own bank will take double the amount and keep all of it in a "holding account" that you do not have access to until your bank is told by the law courts what to do with it. In this way, if you cannot pay your debt, you will have *double the amount of money* that you owe, taken from your bank account, if you set up a direct debit that you cannot later pay. In fact you will be in DOUBLE DEBT.

Interest Free Credit

Interest free credit is another kind of instalment payment plan.

It is an interest free loan. It is similar to **Hire Purchase**, but not the same.

The loan is from a *Credit Company*, also known as a *Finance Company* or *Loan Company*. It means that you get the thing you want, say a bicycle, BUT you get it only by borrowing money from the loan company that the bicycle shop employs.

You pay for the bicycle by spreading out the cost over some months by agreeing to an **instalment payment plan**.

It works like this: you go to a shop and want to buy a bicycle, but you do not pay the whole price immediately, instead you accept the "terms" that the shop offers for **interest free** purchase. Remember – this is a loan. You then must sign a legal agreement that is between you and the shop's finance company, NOT between you and the bicycle shop. The agreement will be for a Direct Debit from your bank account of an agreed amount of money at agreed dates each month. Although **interest free** loans are usually designed to be paid back within a year, the agreement is likely to be for longer, usually for 3 years, which allows time for the Finance Company to collect money from you if you do not pay your debt. If, for example, you do not, for any reason, continue to pay these Direct Debits then the Finance Company will take the following course of action:

1. They will ask you, once, to pay within 10 days of the due date with no penalty.
2. If you still have not paid by the due date, then they will ask again, and this time, and any subsequent times, they will charge you a fee for each month that you do not pay. Fees vary. Before you sign, find out how much this is.
3. If after some months you still have not paid then they will give your name to a debt collector who has the right to go to your house and remove things of equivalent value of the debt that you owe.
4. If you stop paying back the money and still have not paid your debt after a year has passed, then BEWARE because *the* **interest free** *loan changes to an interest bearing loan,* and it will be a HIGH interest rate.

REMEMBER If you do not pay your debts, your name will be on a defaulters list that all banks and loan (finance) companies have access to, so they will always know that you have not paid your debt – in other words – that you have a bad credit history.

THINK TWICE

BEWARE – Many shops that sell through **hire purchase** or with loan **instalment plans** will try to insist that the buyer also buys insurance – don't. The insurance usually covers them, not you, in case you cannot pay the agreed amount of money each month, but YOU have to pay for the insurance which can be expensive. If you need insurance, go to an insurance company, not to a shop that is trying to sell you something.

If the bicycle that you have bought with any of these methods is stolen, even a day after you have bought it, *you still have to pay for it,* so you should have ordinary household insurance against theft.

Beware of "easy" terms. There is almost always a concealed drawback – "a catch". Look very carefully at the terms and conditions. Search for the snags.

> Commercial companies do not have emotions.
> They will not be sorry for you if you cannot pay, as agreed.

Hire purchase / instalment plan payments

Say you pay £40 in the bike shop immediately. This "up front" payment is called a "deposit", and you agree to pay the rest of the cost at the rate of £20 each month. So you will need to make 19 further monthly payments of £20 each. BUT there is a "catch"; you will have to pay extra for the privilege of delaying full payment, and, for spreading them out over the agreed 19 months. The extra will be calculated as a percentage, usually between 10% and 25%. In this case let's suppose it is 20% [20% of 350 = 70], which is added to the original price of the bike of £350, making it a higher total price of £420.

Thus, buying the bicycle will cost £420 using 'hire purchase', instead of £350 when buying it out-right, immediately.

This is the cost of a paying the whole amount on the first day of purchase.

The total cost is £350

By the 16th month the cost of buying with an Instalment Plan has risen above the cost of paying the whole amount on the first day of purchase. Yet, there are still 3 more months to pay.

The total cost is £420

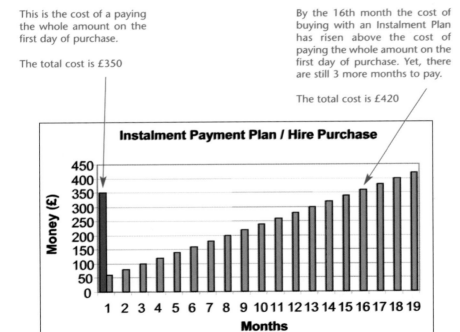

This graph shows the additional cost of spreading-out payments over several months, compared with the cost of paying the whole amount immediately.

Failure to pay hire purchase debts

If you have paid over one third of the full value of the **hire purchase** debt for the things you are buying, but cannot pay the remaining amount, then a court order is essential for the goods to be repossessed. In such a situation bailiffs must get a court order and show it to you, before removing goods.

THINK TWICE

REMEMBER – You pay more if you pay by instalments. It is cheaper to pay the whole amount when you buy something. Some shops do not offer hire purchase terms, but insist on the whole cost of things being paid immediately (up-front).

BE PATIENT – It is cheaper to make yourself wait for something you want, and while you are waiting, save your OWN money each month in your own bank account, then, when you have saved enough to buy the bicycle, pay for it all at once.

You do not have to pay extra, you are not in debt to anyone, and it is yours immediately because you have paid for it all.

You don't need to think about paying anything more.

If you pay the whole cost when you buy it, it is yours forever.

Nobody can take it away.

Don't forget to get a receipt from the bicycle shop – it's proof that the bicycle is yours.

3. Borrowing Money

3.9 Store cards. Shop credit cards. Shop account cards. Charge accounts/credit accounts.

Costs and risks.

VERY EXPENSIVE!	**COST A LOT!**

Some shops, especially multiple or chain-stores, have their own credit cards. You accept the shops' conditions by signing their formal agreements. Shops encourage people to use *their* cards because the interest rate on them is VERY HIGH, which, although good for the shop, is *not good for you*. They work like credit cards BUT are very highly-priced.

Shops sometimes offer special shopping days to their "account holders", and usually a discount, of about 10%, on the first thing you buy, just to entice you. 10% is a good reduction, BUT... **REMEMBER** – Using a **shop credit card** is a way of borrowing money.

THINK TWICE

BEWARE – **Shop cards** cost a lot.

Shops have an APR [Annual Percentage Rate] *much higher* than banks.

This means that the interest charged by the shops is A LOT MORE than the amount of interest charged by banks.

Shops often charge between 29.2% and 30.9% interest, but banks usually charge between 5.9% and 7.3% interest, depending on the circumstances of the borrower, the amount borrowed and the time agreed to pay the money back.

See the sections on overdrafts, on interest and on credit cards.

HIGH CHARGES... COSTLY...

Sometimes shops try to make you use their cards by telling you only their monthly interest charge, but you MUST find out the yearly interest percentage rate – the APR [Annual Percentage Rate] – so that you can compare costs properly.

Shops may charge a monthly fee *in addition* to their VERY HIGH interest rates. *As well as this*, if you use your **shop card** to get money from a cash machine the shop charges you a fee – a high fee. See section 7.8 Loyalty / reward cards.

BEWARE – Some **shop cards** require that you spend a minimum amount each month in their shop. If you do not pay the whole amount off each month when the credit card bill arrives, some shops will charge you *another extra percentage %* on any amount unpaid in your account.

THINK TWICE

Unless you *always pay the whole bill immediately*, using **shop cards** is one of the MOST EXPENSIVE ways to pay for things.

BORROW
£££££££££

PAY BACK
£££££££££££££££££££££££££££

3. Borrowing Money

3.10 Student Loans

How they differ from other loans. Where to find out about them.

A **student loan** is a special kind of loan which is given to students to pay for their education. In order to be eligible for a **student loan**, students must study at an institution that is officially recognised by education authorities. Later, after finishing their course of study, when they get a job, they pay back the money that they have borrowed.

Student loans are different from other loans. They last for a long time and interest rates are lower.

Most students have to borrow money in order to study.

You should apply for a student loan before you start higher education.

A **student loan** is designed to be just enough to live off during term-times as a student. You may have to work during holidays to earn enough money to live off while you are not studying. Many students also need to work part-time during term-time, at the same time as studying. It can be hard work and tiring.

When you have finished your education course, once you have started to earn money, the **student loan** must be paid back. Usually it takes several years to pay back **student loans**, bit by bit.

THINK TWICE

Don't let the prospect of having to pay back a student loan put you off studying the course and getting the qualification that you want. Assess the costs and benefits.

Consider what income you are likely to be able to earn in the future, and how much joy the job will give you as compared, long term, with the amount of satisfaction and money that alternative jobs for unqualified people might bring.

If you are thinking about starting higher education, find out about **student loans**. It will require quite a lot of research to find out all the different possibilities that could help you. Start by asking your school careers advisor, do your research online: there are many websites which provide information; use your local reference library, and seek advice from family and friends.

Not all **student loans** are from government sources. There are also some educational trusts and occasionally even private finance for education, some of which are very specific. Most countries do not require students to start paying back their loans till they earn over a certain amount per year. Each country has different systems and rules.

3. Borrowing Money

3.11 Mortgages

What they are. How they work.

A **mortgage** [known as a **home loan** in North America] is an agreement which allows you to borrow money from a bank or other financial institution, particularly in order to buy a house or flat, or the amount of money itself. This kind of loan is repaid bit by bit every month for many years.

A **bridging loan** [known as a **bridge loan** in North America] is an arrangement in which a bank lends someone some money for a short time until that person can get the money from somewhere else, often so that they can buy another house before they sell the one that they already have.

You get a **mortgage** from building societies, banks, and insurance companies. In North America most house loans are made by "savings-and-loan associations".

A **mortgage** is a very big loan especially for buying houses. People borrow large sums of money with **mortgages** because houses are expensive.

A **mortgage**
is a long-term loan.

It can take a long time, such as 35 years, to pay back, bit by bit.

Each month people pay back a piece of their loan for a house [**mortgage**]. The security or collateral for your **mortgage** is the property itself, which means that until you have paid back ALL of your mortgage, you do not own it, and your house can still be re-possessed by the lender, *if*, and only if, you stop paying your **mortgage**, or do not pay it on time. Some people take out insurance against this happening.

It is the same as not paying back any debt. The lender can take back what ever it is you bought with the borrowed money, or something of equal value. In the case of a **mortgage**, it is unlikely that many people have anything of the same value as their flat or house, so if you do not pay back your **mortgage** on time [default], then lenders can take away your flat [apartment] or house and sell it to someone else.

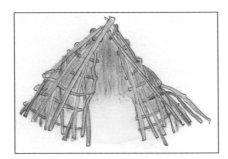

However, people who find that they cannot pay back the cost of their **mortgage**, could sell their property before the **mortgage** company repossesses it, then pay back the whole **mortgage** with the money they get from the sale of their flat or house, then move somewhere cheaper, or rent somewhere to live.

There are many different kinds of **mortgages**, with diverse and differing rates of interest. For example: a fixed rate means that the interest rate, and usually the loan repayment too, remain constant for an agreed length of time, then it changes to a different rate of interest, perhaps to a variable rate.

A variable rate means that the rate of interest can rise or fall depending on Central Banks' fluctuating interest rates and the discretion of the lender.

3. Borrowing Money

3.12 Pawn Shops

What they are. How they work.

 Pawnshops are shops where **pawnbrokers** lend money in exchange for items of personal property, usually jewellery, which can be sold if the owner does not pay an agreed amount of money, plus interest, in an agreed time.

To **pawn** something means to leave something that you own with a **pawnbroker** in exchange for borrowing money. The **pawnbroker** lends you money for an agreed time during which your possession is kept by the **pawnbroker**. People can **pawn** objects of quite small value, and are given a ticket which they use later to redeem (buy back) the thing that they **pawned**.

As soon as the date for redeeming your possession is reached, the **pawnbroker** will sell it. Therefore unless you pay back your debt, within the agreed time, including the interest that the **pawnbroker** charges, about 8%, you will lose the thing that you **pawned**.

Pawnbrokers make money from people who forget to buy back their property, or, who can't afford to pay to get their own things back within the agreed time. The **pawnbroker** can then sell the things at auction for more money than has been lent to the owner.

Some **pawnbrokers** handle gold and silver items only, others accept sports equipment, musical instruments or electronic goods.

THINK TWICE

BEWARE – the percentage charged for electronic goods may be higher, sometimes up to about 25%.

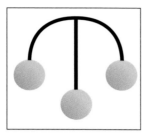

Pawnbrokers' signs are three gold coloured balls. The signs hang outside the pawn shops, which are usually found in areas where people are not rich.

Pawn shops are regulated by local municipal authorities and controlled by the police.

THINK TWICE

BEWARE – You will not get a guarantee on any item bought from **pawn brokers'** shops. Everything is second hand / pre-used / had a previous owner. It is against the law to buy stolen property.

In the past, **pawn brokers** had poor reputations as places where stolen goods were sold. This is changing, but be alert. If something seems an incredible bargain, it is likely to be a bargain that is not credible!

If it seems too good to be true, it probably *is* too good to be true.

3. Borrowing Money

3.13 Credit Cards

What they are. How they work.

Credit cards are small plastic cards with magnetic strips on the back, holographs on the front and electronic computer chips in them which identify your bank account as soon as you enter your secret PIN.

Credit cards are *completely different* from debit cards, because:

- Using a **credit card** is a way of *borrowing money*.
- You spend your bank's money each time you use a **credit card**.
- **Credit cards** cannot be used as cheque guarantee cards.
- **Credit cards** are expensive. The interest rates are high:
  - for cash withdrawals can be up to 24.4% APR.
  - for unpaid bills can be about 20% APR.

Credit cards are designed for paying for things in shops, over the telephone, or on-line, BUT are *very expensive for cash withdrawals*.

There are many **credit card** companies, some are associated with supermarkets others are banks' own. They each have their own interest rate, so look carefully at the small print and compare several rates before you decide what you can afford.

If you use a **credit card**, you will get a bill from your bank at the end of each month. If you pay the whole of this bill within the agreed time, then you will not be charged any interest, if, *and only if*, the interest is on things that you have bought and *not* on withdrawals from cash machines [ATMs].

It *is* possible to withdraw money from cash machines [ATMs] using **credit cards** BUT this is borrowing money and is a *very expensive* way to get cash. Banks always charge interest for withdrawals of any amount of money from cash machines [ATMs] with **credit cards**. Interest on cash withdrawals is higher than for buying things with **credit cards**.

Avoid cash withdrawals	If you *do* use a **credit card** to withdraw money from a cash machine [ATM] you will be charged a "cash handling fee" by banks: usually a small fee on any amount up to about £100, then 2% of any amount over £100.

In addition to this "cash handling fee" you will be charged interest of about 27.7% APR on the amount you withdraw from a cash machine [ATM]. The amount of these percentages changes from time to time, so check them. This interest is charged from the moment you withdraw the cash until the moment the bank puts your payment of their bill into their account. No matter how quickly you pay your **credit card** bill, even if you pay by debit card over the telephone the instant you receive your **credit card** bill, you will *still be charged this interest* on cash withdrawals. There is no way to avoid this high interest charge on cash withdrawals using **credit cards**.

The only way to cut down on the length of time this interest is charged, is to telephone your bank as soon as you have withdrawn money from a cash machine [ATM] with a **credit card** and pay immediately by debit card. Really, there is little point in using a **credit card** to withdraw money from cash machines [ATMs], because it is an expensive way to borrow money from your bank. It is *much cheaper* to use a debit card to withdraw your own money from ATMs.

Buying Things

If you buy things over the phone or on-line you may be asked to give the last three numbers from the series of numbers on the back of your **credit card**. The reason for this is as proof to the seller that you do actually have the card in your hand and are not using a card number that has been stolen. Do not give all the numbers, only the last three digits.

If you buy things with a **credit card** and then do not pay the whole bill within the stated time limit, you will be charged interest. The amount of interest charged depends on the terms of the agreement with each **credit card** company, not on an individual person's credit history, nor on the bank's interest rate unless the **credit card** is the bank's own one. Each **credit card** company can have a different interest rate.

Interest rates can be between about 10% APR and 20% APR. Make certain you know how much your bank intends to charge you, just in case you do not immediately pay back what you have spent buying things with your credit card.

Using a **credit card** is spending the bank's money, *not* yours.

Banks' rates of interest vary, and each bank has slightly different ways of deciding how much interest each individual customer will be charged.

If you do NOT pay the whole amount of a **credit card** bill each month, you will have to pay a larger sum of money overall. That is, the cost of the item you bought, *plus* the interest on any amount unpaid each month. Some banks charge compound interest on unpaid amounts on **credit card** bills, which makes it an expensive way to buy things and to borrow money.

THINK TWICE

REMEMBER – Avoid using **credit cards** to withdraw money from cash machines [ATMs], because you are really borrowing money at a very expensive interest rate.

Pay the whole amount of **credit card** bills each month. Do not merely pay the minimum amount required, because you will be charged high interest on any amount of a **credit card** bill that is not paid.

If, and *only if*, you immediately pay the whole **credit card** bill, as soon as it arrives, and never withdraw cash with a **credit card**, then you can borrow money interest free, for a month at a time, by buying things with it.

Credit card statements/bills are sent every month. To find out about how they work, and how to pay them, see Section 3.14 credit card bills.

Some banks offer several different **credit cards**. They do this in the expectation that you will get into debt, and will have to pay them interest and overdraft charges. That is partly how banks make money.

One **credit card** is sufficient.
If you can't pay back the money you owe on one card immediately, *do not* get another, instead, pay back the debt.

Other than keeping one separate **credit card** for paying for things on the net, so as to keep close track of it, there is no reason to have several **credit cards**. The more credit cards you have, the more the bills YOU have to pay, and the more opportunity fraudsters have to rob you.

If a **credit card** offers "interest free terms", make sure that you know how long the interest "free" time lasts and on which transactions it is available.

BEWARE – Banks need to make money, and YOU are *forever* responsible for paying back money that you spend using a **credit card**.

Check all letters from your bank very carefully, including all the small print. **Credit card** companies frequently make changes in **credit card** rules and conditions. Watch out for changes in such things as late payment fees, balance transfer fees, minimum repayment percentages and APRs.

Read the terms and conditions from your **credit card** company, so as to make sure you know what you are paying for.

Banks tend to encourage you to get into debt, making it seem acceptable to spend with borrowed money, but loans are liabilities.

DEBT CAN RUIN YOUR LIFE

The money that you spend when you use **credit cards** is borrowed, whether you spread it out over several **credit cards**, or "consolidate" it into one, makes no difference, it is still debt that YOU have to pay back.

3. Borrowing Money

3.14 Credit Card Bills / Statements

How they work. How to decipher them.
How to pay them. Risks. Examples. Balance transfers.
What they are. How to do It. Pros and cons.

Credit card bills are sent every month. They show how much money you have borrowed by spending with a credit card. They look like this:

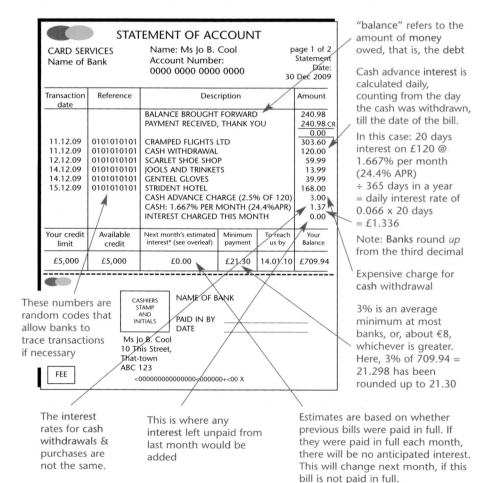

STATEMENT OF ACCOUNT

CARD SERVICES
Name of Bank

Name: Ms Jo B. Cool
Account Number:
0000 0000 0000 0000

page 1 of 2
Statement
Date:
30 Dec 2009

Transaction date	Reference	Description	Amount
		BALANCE BROUGHT FORWARD	240.98
		PAYMENT RECEIVED, THANK YOU	240.98 CR
			0.00
11.12.09	0101010101	CRAMPED FLIGHTS LTD	303.60
11.12.09	0101010101	CASH WITHDRAWAL	120.00
12.12.09	0101010101	SCARLET SHOE SHOP	59.99
14.12.09	0101010101	JOOLS AND TRINKETS	13.99
14.12.09	0101010101	GENTEEL GLOVES	39.99
15.12.09	0101010101	STRIDENT HOTEL	168.00
		CASH ADVANCE CHARGE (2.5% OF 120)	3.00
		CASH: 1.667% PER MONTH (24.4%APR)	1.37
		INTEREST CHARGED THIS MONTH	0.00

Your credit limit	Available credit	Next month's estimated interest* (see overleaf)	Minimum payment	To reach us by	Your Balance
£5,000	£5,000	£0.00	£21.30	14.01.10	£709.94

CASHIERS STAMP AND INITIALS

NAME OF BANK

PAID IN BY
DATE _____

Ms Jo B. Cool
10 This Street,
That-town
ABC 123

FEE

<000000000000000-000000+<00 X

"balance" refers to the amount of money owed, that is, the debt

Cash advance interest is calculated daily, counting from the day the cash was withdrawn, till the date of the bill.

In this case: 20 days interest on £120 @ 1.667% per month (24.4% APR)
÷ 365 days in a year
= daily interest rate of 0.066 x 20 days
= £1.336

Note: Banks round *up* from the third decimal

Expensive charge for cash withdrawal

3% is an average minimum at most banks, or, about €8, whichever is greater. Here, 3% of 709.94 = 21.298 has been rounded up to 21.30

These numbers are random codes that allow banks to trace transactions if necessary

The interest rates for cash withdrawals & purchases are not the same.

This is where any interest left unpaid from last month would be added

Estimates are based on whether previous bills were paid in full. If they were paid in full each month, there will be no anticipated interest. This will change next month, if this bill is not paid in full.

With **credit card statements**, many credit card companies send a "Summary of Account". It looks like this:

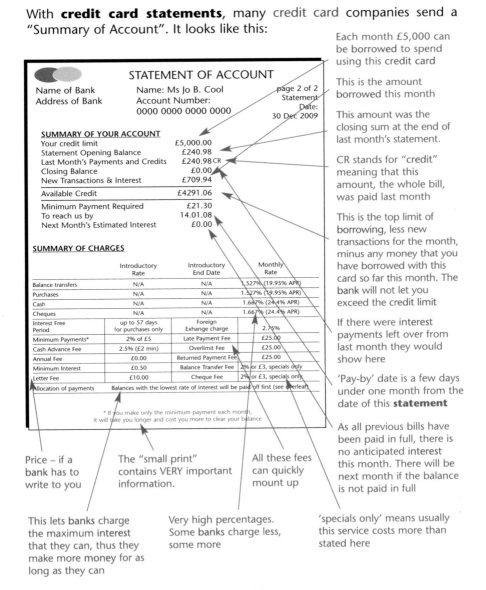

Each month £5,000 can be borrowed to spend using this credit card

This is the amount borrowed this month

This amount was the closing sum at the end of last month's statement.

CR stands for "credit" meaning that this amount, the whole bill, was paid last month

This is the top limit of borrowing, less new transactions for the month, minus any money that you have borrowed with this card so far this month. The bank will not let you exceed the credit limit

If there were interest payments left over from last month they would show here

'Pay-by' date is a few days under one month from the date of this **statement**

As all previous bills have been paid in full, there is no anticipated interest this month. There will be next month if the balance is not paid in full

Price – if a bank has to write to you

The "small print" contains VERY important information.

All these fees can quickly mount up

This lets banks charge the maximum interest that they can, thus they make more money for as long as they can

Very high percentages. Some banks charge less, some more

'specials only' means usually this service costs more than stated here

Look carefully at the very bottom of this.

In very small print is a crucial bit of information: paying minimum monthly payments only, raises the overall cost – MUCH HIGHER. Banks do not print this vital information in large print because they want you to pay interest to them.

It is one of the ways that banks make money.

If you do not pay any amount of a **credit card bill**, the balance that you owe will be moved (carried-over) to next month's bill, PLUS more interest because you did not pay. If you do not pay at all for 3 months, you will be "in default" = a non-payer. Banks will employ a debt collector to get their money back.

REMEMBER – Keep old **credit card bills** for a year, then shred them before you throw them away. This makes your financial identity more difficult for thieves to find, if they were to raid your rubbish bin / trash can to try to steal it.

Banks make money from customers who are in debt.

People who do not pay off the whole amount of their **credit card** debts each month, but instead pay only the minimum amount required, usually have to pay penalty charges too.

These people, who are debtors, are called "revolvers" by banks because they are continuously in debt, and never pay back all the money they owe; they rotate their debts back into the banks' interest gathering system every month.

Banks want to keep such customers because they make money from them, so they will offer more loans, and keep raising credit limits, tempting people into debt.

THINK TWICE

Take notice of what is happening on your **credit card** bills. If you are unsure who has charged your card, make sure you query that transaction.

It's *really* easy to drift casually into debt without being properly aware of it.

Take control of your money – thus, of your life.

BEWARE – It is not in the slightest bit difficult to get into worse debt

£$¥€£$¥€£

If you repay only the 'minimum required payment' on **credit card** bills, you are doing three things:

1. delaying paying back your debt.
2. deciding to *pay more overall*, because you will be charged interest which will increase each month.
3. increasing the length of time it takes to pay off your debt. The smaller the sum you pay back each month, the longer it takes to pay it all back.

THINK TWICE

REMEMBER – The minimum amount may not even cover the interest for one month, far less pay off the debt. It can take 10, 15 or 20 *years* to pay back one month's **credit card** debt, *if* you pay only the minimum amount required per month.

Paying only the 'minimum required payments' of **credit card** bills is almost like giving a present of your money to a bank.

DEBTS EASILY GROW

Balance Transfer Form

Some banks send 'balance transfer forms' with **credit card bills**. They look like this:

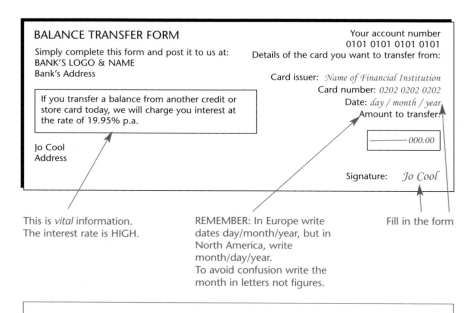

BALANCE TRANSFER FORM

Simply complete this form and post it to us at:
BANK'S LOGO & NAME
Bank's Address

Your account number
0101 0101 0101 0101
Details of the card you want to transfer from:

Card issuer: *Name of Financial Institution*
Card number: *0202 0202 0202*
Date: *day / month / year*
Amount to transfer:

If you transfer a balance from another credit or store card today, we will charge you interest at the rate of 19.95% p.a.

Jo Cool
Address

——— 000.00

Signature: *Jo Cool*

This is *vital* information.
The interest rate is HIGH.

REMEMBER: In Europe write dates day/month/year, but in North America, write month/day/year.
To avoid confusion write the month in letters not figures.

Fill in the form

Note that it does not tell you how much
the Balance Transfer Fee is

Transferring balances is the process of moving an unpaid credit card debt, called an **'outstanding balance'** – from one credit card to another. People usually do it to get a lower interest rate on their debts.

BEWARE – Banks usually charge a 'Balance Transfer Fee'. Find out how much your bank charges for this service. It might be HIGH.

Interest rates can change, even within one month. If you transfer an **outstanding balance** to a lower interest bearing credit card, it may remain at that interest level for a short time only. Card issuers may offer lower "introductory" interest rates to encourage **balance transfers** in, but charge fees to discourage them from being taken out. This means that you have to keep a regular watch on what rate of interest you are being charged.

REMEMBER – Moving a debt (outstanding balance) does not pay back the debt. It just moves it to another place. You still have to pay off the debt.

3. Borrowing Money

3.15 Credit Limits

What They Are. How To Manage Them.

Credit cards have **credit limits**, which is the maximum amount of money that your bank will allow you to borrow each month by spending with your credit card. If you spend more than the **credit limit** you will be charged VERY high interest. Your **credit limit** is written on your credit card statements.

Banks will try to flatter you by raising your credit limit, but BEWARE... don't be fooled into believing that your bank necessarily thinks that you are able to *pay back* a larger amount each month. Banks deliberately raise **credit limits** on credit cards so as to encourage you to spend more, hoping that you will get into debt and then have to pay interest to them. This is one of the ways that banks make money.

PLATINUM   GOLD

If a bank offers you a gold card or a platinum card, which have higher **credit limits**, it does not necessarily mean that you are able to use it. Before spending, pause, and ask yourself:

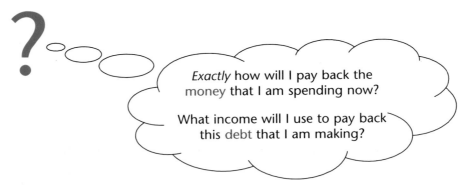

Exactly how will I pay back the money that I am spending now?

What income will I use to pay back this debt that I am making?

REMEMBER – using a credit card is borrowing money, no matter what the **credit limit** is. Whatever you spend with a credit card MUST be paid back. YOU must pay it back.

Credit card cheques

Some banks issue **credit card cheques**. They are VERY EXPENSIVE ways of writing cheques. They are not like normal cheques because all spending with credit cards is borrowing, so, the amount that the cheques are written for has to be paid back each month, if not, you will be charged interest. Usually the interest charged for **credit card cheques** is about 22% APR charged daily. Check this by looking at your credit agreement that comes with your credit card statement.

Sometimes credit card companies offer a lower "promotional" or "introductory"percentage rate, but BEWARE, these are short term and quickly revert to full interest rate.

THINK TWICE

Credit card cheques look very similar, but are VERY different to current account cheques.

4. Making Money

4.1 Income

What it is. Different kinds.

Income is money that is earned from doing work, or, received from investments.

> **Income** is any money that you receive.

Earned income is the money you get from working for it.

Private income, [sometimes called "private means"] is also known as **"unearned income"**. It is money that does not come from doing a job. It might come from family, or, is paid through dividends from investments, or from rent that is paid by people who live in a property that you own.

Most personal **income** is taxable. That tax is called **income** tax. You *must* pay it. Governments decide in what way, and how much, citizens are taxed.

Different countries have different systems of taxing **income**. Usually people with higher **incomes** pay proportionately more tax than those with lower **incomes**.

Business / corporate **income** is also taxable. The rates of tax are different for individuals than for businesses.

Gross Income – is **income** before tax.

Net Income – is **income** after tax.

Disposable income is the amount of your money that you can spend in whatever way you want, on things that are not necessities. It is for luxuries and FUN...

You have a choice over what to do with the money that is left after you have paid tax, for food or other essential things that you need in order to live.

Assessable income is the amount of money that is considered, or assessed, by tax authorities when they calculate how much tax you have to pay.

4. Making Money

4.2 Earn

Fringe benefit. Overtime. What they are.

To **earn** money is to be paid money for work.

Earnings are the amount of money that people get paid for working.

Some earning terms

A **bonus** is an extra amount of money that is sometimes paid, if employees work very well, or quickly. Some companies pay their workers **bonuses** at Christmas, at the end of a project, or, at the end of a year of business.

A **commission** is a percentage, royalty, or fee that is paid by employers in return for sales success.

A **fringe benefit** is an advantage, perk or extra something that people get because of their job. It is not money. It is something in addition to money earned. It could be a company car; a pension plan; profit-sharing; insurance for health, life or unemployment; reduced fees for membership of a gym; free or reduced travel costs; subsidised petrol costs, or even good loan rates.

It could also be lunch-vouchers, or a canteen at work that is free or cheap; or the privilege of being allowed to use the company swimming pool.

Overtime

Employees can sometimes choose to work for more time than the standard number of hours for which they are employed. This extra time is called **overtime**. It is usually worked after normal working hours, perhaps at night or at weekends. If people choose to work extra hours, they might be paid **overtime** rates. Usually **overtime** rates are higher than the standard rate of pay per hour.

OVERTIME over the normal rate paid for time spent working

Workers might be paid **overtime** rates of:

– "time and a half"; meaning that they get paid the normal rate of pay, *plus* half of the normal rate per hour.
– "Double time" is twice the normal hourly rate of pay.

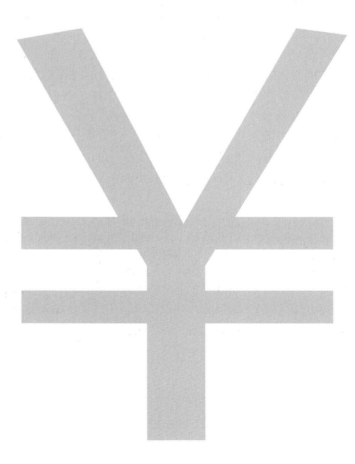

4. Making Money

4.3 Salary

Payment types. Examples. Definitions.

If you have a job, you get paid for your work. You earn your own money which is called a **salary** or a **wage**. They are fixed amounts of money agreed in advance, usually paid directly into the employee's bank account every month.

A **starting salary** is the amount of money that employees get when starting a particular type of job for the first time. It's usually a small one.

A **basic salary** is what a person earns before other sums of money are added or removed – such as overtime extra and tax deductions. **Gross salary** is before tax and **net salary** is after tax.

Usually a **salary** is paid for long term or non-physical work, for which people need years of education and training.

Most employers pay **salaries** with the direct credit [direct deposit] method.

When you get paid for working, you get a **wage** or **salary** slip which gives information about how much you are being paid each month, how much you have been paid so far each financial year, and what tax you must pay.

A payslip shows details about how you are paid

It looks something like the example over the page.

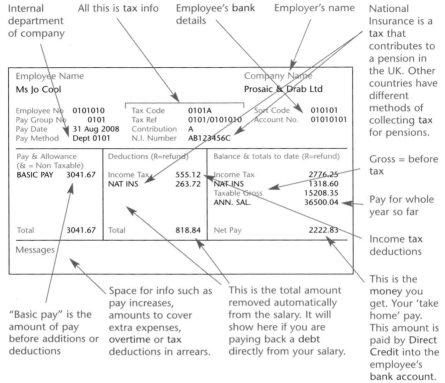

Internal department of company

All this is tax info

Employee's bank details

Employer's name

National Insurance is a tax that contributes to a pension in the UK. Other countries have different methods of collecting tax for pensions.

Gross = before tax

Pay for whole year so far

Income tax deductions

This is the money you get. Your 'take home' pay. This amount is paid by Direct Credit into the employee's bank account.

"Basic pay" is the amount of pay before additions or deductions

Space for info such as pay increases, amounts to cover extra expenses, overtime or tax deductions in arrears.

This is the total amount removed automatically from the salary. It will show here if you are paying back a debt directly from your salary.

Employee Name			Company Name	
Ms Jo Cool			Prosaic & Drab Ltd	
Employee No	0101010	Tax Code	0101A	Sort Code	010101
Pay Group No	0101	Tax Ref	0101/0101010	Account No.	01010101
Pay Date	31 Aug 2008	Contribution	A		
Pay Method	Dept 0101	N.I. Number	AB123456C		

Pay & Allowance (& = Non Taxable)		Deductions (R=refund)		Balance & totals to date (R=refund)	
BASIC PAY	3041.67	Income Tax	555.12	Income Tax	2776.25
		NAT INS	263.72	NAT INS	1318.60
				Taxable Gross	15208.35
				ANN. SAL.	36500.04
Total	3041.67	Total	818.84	Net Pay	2222.83
Messages					

Wage

In Australia and New Zealand a **wage** is known as a "check".

A **wage** is money that usually paid for physical work that requires strength, skill or dexterity, rather than higher education.

Temporary workers are paid **wages**. The amount of a **wage** is usually calculated per hour or per week, not per month. **Wages** are usually paid each week, although sometimes **wages** are paid per month.

A **minimum wage** is the smallest amount of money that a government allows an employer to pay anyone who works for them.

A **wage packet** [called **"paycheck"** in North America] is the money that you earn, especially when it is given to you in notes and coins in an envelope.

A **wage freeze** is a stop on rises and falls in **wages**, sometimes called **wage fixing**, so that they remain at a particular level. A **wage freeze** is controlled by a company or government.

4. Making Money

4.4 Business Terms

Entrepreneur

An **entrepreneur** is a person who organises, starts and often also owns a business.

They are usually enterprising people who start new businesses and take financial risks, hoping that if a business succeeds, they will make a profit.

Someone with an **entrepreneurial** spirit is a person who is likely to make money.

Limited company

A **limited company**, written as "Ltd.", is one that has legally limited liability, that is, the owners are liable for debts up to a certain limit only.

It is a way of protecting owners of businesses from loosing everything they have, if their business company goes bankrupt.

If the company makes a loss and fails financially, only the business will be lost but the individual will not lose all her/his possessions. The capital invested in the business, but not the personal assets of the owner, are liable to assessment by the authorities for business debts that must be paid. It is a way of minimizing risk to individuals.

Turnover

Turnover is *not* the same as profit. **Turnover** is the amount of business that a company does in a period of time, and is also used to mean the number and value of shares traded on a stock exchange.

Turnover is the sequence of sale and replacement of goods through a business.

It can also refer to the movement of people – employees – in and out of a company.

Sometimes even if profit is not high, **turnover** can be large.

Turnover minus costs = profit.

When all the costs have been paid, *then* tax has to be paid, then, what is left at the end of the whole process, is profit.

For a business to be successful, **turnover** is designed ...along an extensive route... to lead to profit.

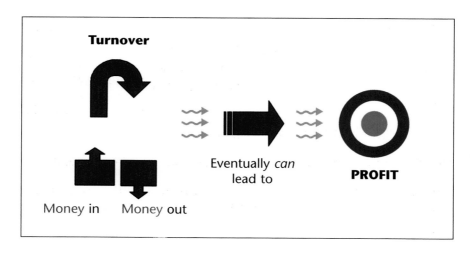

4. Making Money

4.5 Profit

What it is. How it is reached. Example.

> **Profit** is income, and so it is taxable.
>
> **Profit** is the difference between the costs of getting and making something and the amount of money earned from selling it.

If you buy something for 10 and sell it for 10.5 then you have made 0.5 **profit**, BUT if you buy for 10 and sell for 10.5 AND have 0.3 expenses for storing or transporting the item, then your **profit** will be 0.2.

For example:

If a bicycle factory has to pay:

    £60 for the parts of a bicycle
    £130 to make a bicycle & pay people to make it
    £5 for insurance of the factory where it is made
    £10 to deliver it, with others, to the bicycle shop
= £205

plus, 20% tax = £41 [205 + 41] = £246 per bicycle.

So... the whole cost to the factory of making one bicycle is £246.00

If the bicycle factory then adds a percentage for **profit**, based on the total cost of producing a bike, say 5% [5% of £246 = 12.30]

£246 + 12.30 = £258.30

This means that the bicycle factory sells each bike for £258.30.

The bicycle factory's **profit** on each bike is = £12.30

Sell bike for   =   £258.30
Make bike for =   £246.00
                  £12.30

A **profit margin** is a precise financial measurement that is calculated by dividing profit by sales. Here, the **profit margin** is:

£12.30 (profit) ÷ £258.30 (selling price) = 4.8%

If, and only if, your bicycle factory can make *and* sell 200 bikes a day, every day, then each day it will make a **profit** of £2,460

BUT...   what if the tax is raised? Or insurance costs go up?
- or   the roof of the factory has to be repaired?
- or   one of the bicycle making machines breaks down?
- or   two highly trained bike makers fall ill and can't work for 3 weeks?
- or   fashion changes so different bikes start to sell, so you have to redesign?
- or   there is a delay in supply of spare parts, so production stops for a month?

The next thing in supply of bicycles, is that the bicycle shop has to sell them at a price to cover *their* costs – of renting the shop, peoples' wages, telephones and so on – *and* the bicycle shop has to make a **profit** too.

So, the bicycle shop adds 20% of the cost of buying the bike from the factory [20% of £258.30 = £51.66]

£258.30 + £51.66 = £309.96

Thus, the bicycle shop makes money to cover its costs and to make a profit.

All this makes the bicycle that is for sale in the bicycle shop cost you (the buyer), £309.96

Unfortunately, profit does *not* rain from the sky!

Profit sharing is a system of sharing the **profits** that a company makes between all the people who work for it.

Paper profit is the **profit** that is shown in financial records but which has not yet been made by a company, because it is waiting for payments it is owed.

A **not-for-profit** or **non-profit-making** organisation is one that deliberately does not make **profit**. **Non-profit** organisations are usually charities, or Development Organisations such as Non Governmental Organisations (NGOs), and often can be eligible for tax relief.

THINK TWICE

BEWARE – **Profit** is not the same as *profiteering*.

Profiteering is making money through exploitation.

A "profiteer" is a disapproving way of describing a person who takes advantage of a situation in which other people are suffering to make a **profit**, often by selling goods which are difficult to obtain at a high price.

4. Making Money

4.6 Break even

What is it. Graph example.

> To **break even** is to have no profit or loss.
>
> **Breaking even** happens when a business earns enough money to pay for expenses, without any profit. It is the point just before profit starts, when income equals costs, that is, zero profit and zero loss.

It is an important figure for anyone who manages a business because the **break-even point** is the lower limit of profit when setting prices and working out profit margins.

After the **breakeven point** is when the profit starts; that is, the amount by which costs differ from the amount of money earned from sales.

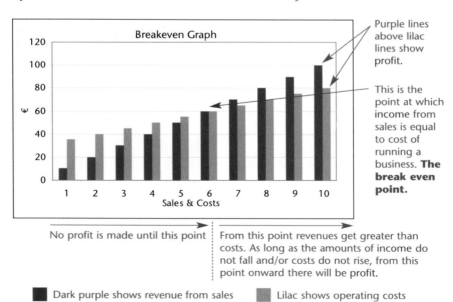

Purple lines above lilac lines show profit.

This is the point at which income from sales is equal to cost of running a business. **The break even point.**

No profit is made until this point ⋮ From this point revenues get greater than costs. As long as the amounts of income do not fall and/or costs do not rise, from this point onward there will be profit.

■ Dark purple shows revenue from sales ▨ Lilac shows operating costs

Revenues from sales grow faster than costs, over time.

4. Making Money

4.7 Money from other sources – dividends

What they are. Who gets them.

A **dividend** is part of the profit of a company that is paid to people who have bought shares. These people are called shareholders.

a share

A **dividend** is the amount of money per share of a company's profit which is paid to shareholders.

Usually **dividends** are paid once each year. **Dividends** can be paid more frequently, if so, they are called "interim **dividends**".

Shareholders in a company may be paid **dividends**, if, and only if, the company declares that it will pay dividends, and makes a profit.

Dividends are unearned income, and taxable.

4. Making Money

4.8 Money from other sources – inherited money

What is it. Who gets it.

Everyone will die sometime.

It is sensible to think carefully what you want to be done with your money and possessions, after you are dead. If you want to be sure that people will do what you want with your possessions when you are dead, write a "will", which is a legal document giving details of who will **inherits** what.

To **inherit** means to receive money or things from someone who has died.

An **inheritance** is money or things that have been given by someone who is dead.

An **inheritor** is a person who has been left something in someone's will.

A *legacy* is the name for the money or things that have been inherited.

A *legatee* is someone to whom a legacy is given.

5. Keeping Money

Part 1: Recording and Managing Money

5.1 Debit

What is it. Where to find it.

> **Debit** is *not* exactly the same as debt.
>
> Both are minus [negative] amounts of money.
>
> All businesses must keep records of financial information either on a computer or on paper.
>
> To **debit** a sum of money is part of the act of writing down financial information in a special kind of commercial documentation.

The special system for recording this information is called **book-keeping**. Skilled people, called **accountants**, or "auditors", maintain systematic records of money in a business, and prepare precise information to give to tax authorities. Each country has laws about how this has to be done.

There are several different software packages for recording and managing money, some are for business accounting and others are more useful for managing personal **accounts**.

accounts
a statement of monetary transactions

A **ledger** is the main book in which the business transactions of a company are recorded. Sometimes it is called an "account book".

Two columns of figures are written in **ledgers**.

A **debit** is the column of figures on the left side of a **ledger**. It shows amounts of money that has been spent.

Debit can be described as recording of items of debt in a **ledger**.

DEBIT

CREDIT

credit

any entry of a sum of money on the right hand side of an account

accrual

an allowance made for a transaction known to be due, but not yet finalised

depreciation

the reduced accounting value of something you own

Recording financial information

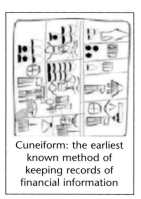

Cuneiform: the earliest known method of keeping records of financial information

Feather quill pen

Braille keyboard

THINK TWICE

BEWARE – **Debit** can also be used to describe the way that banks record money that has been taken out of a bank account. Money is **debited** from accounts.

If a bank account is in **debit**, it means that more money has been spent than was in that account at the time. The account will then be overdrawn, and in debt.

5. Keeping Money

5.2 Budget

What it is

> A **budget** is a financial plan that shows how much money you expect or need to spend over a specific time, AND it shows how much income you expect to have for that particular time.

To **budget** is to plan how much money you will spend on particular things. Businesses **budget** to make sure they keep to their plans and make profits.

A personal **budget** is useful because it tells you exactly how much you have, how much you will need to spend on essential things and how much will be left over.

See section 5.4 End of Month Reckoning – Balancing Your Budget

The money you get MUST be more than the money you spend, or, you'll fall... into debt.

 **The Budget** is the official statement that a government makes about how much money it will collect in taxes and spend on public services in the future.

Usually the Minister of Finance /Chancellor of the Exchequer announces **The Budget** for the coming fiscal year in parliament.

5. Keeping Money

5.3 Receipt

What it is. Examples. Risks.

A **receipt** is sometimes called a "**sales slip**". It is a document that proves that you have bought something. Shops, restaurants and even on-line companies must provide receipts. Make sure that you are given a **receipt** for everything that you buy.

Receipts show the following information:

- Date – and sometimes time too.
- How much you spent.
- Where you shopped – the name and sometimes address of the shop.
- What you bought – sometimes the **receipt** does not tell you exactly what you bought, but just a vague description, or a short version of the name of a product, and often the shop's product code is included.

Here is an example of a typical food shop **receipt**:

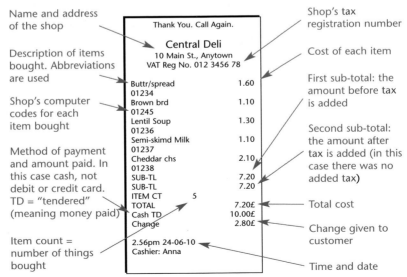

Name and address of the shop

Description of items bought. Abbreviations are used

Shop's computer codes for each item bought

Method of payment and amount paid. In this case cash, not debit or credit card. TD = "tendered" (meaning money paid)

Item count = number of things bought

Shop's tax registration number

Cost of each item

First sub-total: the amount before tax is added

Second sub-total: the amount after tax is added (in this case there was no added tax)

Total cost

Change given to customer

Time and date

```
Thank You. Call Again.

      Central Deli
    10 Main St., Anytown
   VAT Reg No. 012 3456 78

Buttr/spread          1.60
01234
Brown brd             1.10
01245
Lentil Soup           1.30
01236
Semi-skimd Milk       1.10
01237
Cheddar chs           2.10
01238
SUB-TL                7.20
SUB-TL                7.20
ITEM CT       5
TOTAL                7.20£
Cash TD             10.00£
Change               2.80£

2.56pm 24-06-10
Cashier: Anna
```

Keep all receipts, take them home and put them safely in an envelope marked with the month and year, till the end of the month when you check what you have spent in your end of month Financial Reckoning. In this way you'll know whether there has been any fraud attempted on your bank account.

A **receipt** for something more expensive might look like this:

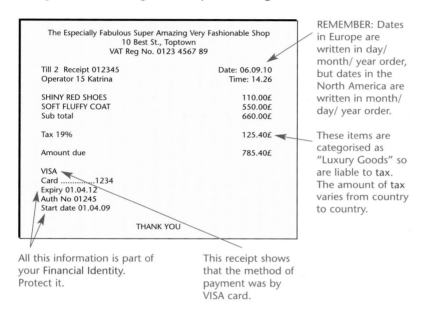

The Especially Fabulous Super Amazing Very Fashionable Shop
10 Best St., Toptown
VAT Reg No. 0123 4567 89

Till 2 Receipt 012345   Date: 06.09.10
Operator 15 Katrina   Time: 14.26

SHINY RED SHOES   110.00£
SOFT FLUFFY COAT   550.00£
Sub total   660.00£

Tax 19%   125.40£

Amount due   785.40£

VISA
Card 1234
Expiry 01.04.12
Auth No 01245
Start date 01.04.09

THANK YOU

REMEMBER: Dates in Europe are written in day/ month/ year order, but dates in the North America are written in month/ day/ year order.

These items are categorised as "Luxury Goods" so are liable to tax. The amount of tax varies from country to country.

All this information is part of your Financial Identity. Protect it.

This receipt shows that the method of payment was by VISA card.

If you take something that you do not want back to the shop where you bought it, and show your **receipt**, sometimes, instead of getting your money back, you might be given a **credit note**. A **credit note** is a piece of paper that allows you to buy other things up to the same value in that shop. It is a way for shops to make sure that you spend your money in *their* shop, and not elsewhere; in this way they do not loose money, if you return something.

You need **receipts** to claim income tax relief and expenses from your employer.

THINK TWICE

REMEMBER - Do not throw away **receipts** until you have checked them in your end of month Financial Reckoning. Keep **receipts** for expensive things, such as electronics, in case there is a defect and something has to be taken back to a shop. Some people keep them until they get rid of the equipment. **Receipts** for large amounts should be kept for 6 years and those for major financial commitments, such as life insurance, should be kept for 4 years after you have paid all the money.

THINK TWICE

BEWARE – When the time comes to throw away old **receipts** ALWAYS rip them into small pieces, or shred them, so that your Financial Identity cannot be found.

Note:
Rules for receipts for personal purchases may be different to those for business. For work receipts, ask your employer.

---

5. Keeping Money

5.4 Monthly Financial Reckoning/Budgeting

2 + 2 = 4		8 − 2 = 6
4 + 2 = 6	**ADD IT**	6 − 2 = 4
6 + 2 = 8		4 − 2 = 2
8 + 2 = 10	**ALL UP**	2 − 2 = 0
10 + 2 = 12		0 − 2 = −2

How To Do It. When To Do It. Example. Risks.

Calculate your costs

Get into the habit of checking your finances at the end of each month.

It doesn't take long and is important because you are more likely to spot fraud if you get used to seeing what happens to your money and how your accounts work.

Throughout each month, as you get receipts, pop them into a folder, along with any other notes to yourself about your finances; then, when your bank statement arrives, sort them all out.

Assess your Budget

So that you always know how much money you have, throughout each month, keep a record of what you spend, as you spend it, with a list something like this:

Date	What Bought	Where	Amount spent
1.04.09	monthly bus ticket	Bus station	£25.00
2.04.09	soap, toothpaste etc	Cough Pharmacy	£11.25
5.04.09	train ticket	on-line: Quick Trains	£32.49
12.04.09	bicycle	Coolest Bikes ltd	£250.00
20.04.09	DVDs	Soaring Sounds	£19.99
24.04.09	M's birthday present	Super Special Stuff	£29.95
29.04.09	Sweets	newsagent	£2.48
30.04.09	pen & photocopies	school shop	£3.08

...and so on, till the end of the month, then add it all up   TOTAL =   £374.24

Work out how much you spend

This is a simple quick way to keep track of how much you spend, on what, where and when. Some people do this with software on a computer.

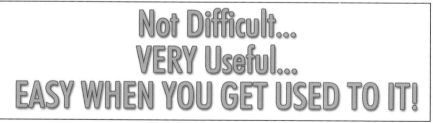

Not Difficult...
VERY Useful...
EASY WHEN YOU GET USED TO IT!

At the end of each month your bank will send you a statement.

- Take all of the receipts from the last month, look through the statement and check each item on your statement against the receipts.
- Tick each receipt that is correctly listed on your statement and tick each item on your statement that matches with each receipt.
- Check dates and amounts of money.

Remember that not all items on your statement will have receipts for them. For example Standing Orders or Direct Debits will not have receipts, nor will withdrawals from ATMs.

Each month look carefully at your accounts IT ONLY TAKES 10 MINUTES...

THINK TWICE

BEWARE – Make sure that there are no amounts on your statement that you do not know about.

If you see any item for any amount of money, no matter how small, that you did not take out of your account, then assume that a fraudster has started to cheat you.

Fraudsters quite often start by cheating people of small amounts of money, hoping that it will not be noticed. Later, in another month, they may make larger withdrawals, thus cheating you of even more money.

If you think that there is a possibility that there has been a fraudulent attempt to take money from your account, telephone your bank and tell them what you suspect.

It is important to tell your bank *as soon as you notice* anything suspicious, so that they can investigate, and so that you will not be forced to pay for the amounts that thieves have tried to steal from you.

balance your budget

ASK YOURSELF:

How much money is coming in?
How much money is going out?

5. Keeping Money

Part 2: Saving and Investing Money

5.5 Capital / Principal

What it is. Definitions.

> A main or primary amount of money or property is a **capital** or **principal** amount, and it contrasts with the income derived from it. Savings make up part of a person's **capital**.
>
> **Capital** or **principal** is the original amount from which interest is obtained. It is also the original amount on which calculations are made for payment of interest on a debt.

See section 3.2 Interest.

capital (MONEY)
wealth, especially a large amount of money used for producing more wealth or for starting a new business: *She leaves her capital untouched in the bank and lives off the interest.*

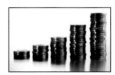

capitalize, UK USUALLY SPELT capitalise
to supply money to a business so that it can develop or operate as it should

capitalization, UK USUALLY SPELT capitalisation
the total value of a company's shares on a *stock exchange*

capital assets
the buildings and machines owned by a business or other organization

capital gains
profits made by selling property or an investment

capital gains tax (ALSO CDT)
tax on the profits made from selling something you own

capital intensive
describes an industry, business or process that needs a lot of money to buy buildings and equipment in order to start operating: *As agriculture became more capital intensive, many farm labourers moved to the towns and cities to look for work.*

capital investment (ALSO capital expenditure)
money which is spent on buildings and equipment to increase the effectiveness of a business

venture capital
money that is invested or is available for investment in a new company, especially a risky one: *They'll need to raise £1 million in venture capital if they're to get the business off the ground.*

working capital
the money belonging to a company which is immediately available for business use, rather than money it has in investments or property

capital assets
the buildings and machines owned by a business or other organization

5. Keeping Money

5.6 Stocks and Shares

What They Are. Who Gets Them. Definitions.

A **share** is ownership of part of a business company. Businesses and ownerships of companies are divided up into **shares**. Each **share** can be bought by members of the public. People can own tiny amounts of a company.

...a share...

A **stock** is the amount of money which a company has by selling **shares** to people. It is also part of the ownership of a company which people buy as an investment.

A **shareholder** or **stockholder** is a person who owns some of the equal parts into which the ownership of a company is divided.

Government bonds are types of stock that produce a fixed rate of interest for a defined time span. They are issued by a government and return of capital is guaranteed.

Stock exchanges or **stock markets** are places where **stockbrokers** buy and sell **stocks** and **shares**. They vary in value and can go up ▲, or down ▼.

People guess, based on their knowledge and experience, whether the value of **stocks** will go up ▲, or down ▼.

Stockbrokers are people, or companies, that try to make money by buying and selling **stocks** and **shares**. Often they do this for other people or with other peoples' money. Some people say that they gamble on **stocks** and **shares**. It is a risky business.

greed

Stock markets are said to be influenced by **stockbrokers'** greed and fear in equal proportions; sometimes one has influence and sometimes the other.

fear

A "bearish" **stockbroker** expects a fall in **stock** prices. They sell **shares** when prices are expected to fall, hoping that they can make a profit by buying them back again later, at a lower price.

Bear market

A "bullish" **stockbroker** expects a rise in **stock** prices. They buy **shares** expecting prices will rise, hoping that they can make profit by selling them later for more money than they paid for them.

Bull market

The biggest stock markets in the world are in:

London, UK;

Frankfurt, Germany;

Tokyo, Japan;

New York, USA;

and there are smaller ones elsewhere.

THINK TWICE

Stocks and **Shares** can fall in value. You can lose money. You can lose *all the money you invest.*

Invest – To **invest** means to choose to put money into a business or shares, for the purpose of making a profit.

Speculation – To **speculate** is a kind of investment that involves high risk but also the possibility of high profits. Some people describe it as a kind of gambling.

5. Keeping Money

5.7 Pension

What it is. Who gets it.

A **pension** is money that is paid regularly by a government or a private company to people who do not work any more, perhaps because they are too old to work, or, maybe they are not healthy enough to work, or, some people may have an accident and have been seriously injured, so that work is impossible.

THINK TWICE

BEWARE – **Pensions** have to be saved for.

People save money for their old age while they are working earning money.

They usually save some of their money each month for many years, so that they will have enough to live off in times when they cannot work. Sometimes they pay into a **pension fund**.

A **pension fund** / **pension plan** / **pension scheme** is a financial plan for saving money that allows you to receive money later, after you or your employer has paid into it for many years.

Usually **pension schemes** are designed so that many people can pay into a particular **pension savings plan** for many years, especially employees of a company. Money is invested in order to provide them with a **pension** when they are older.

A person of **pensionable** age is someone who is old enough to claim a **pension**.

A **pensioner** is a person who receives a **pension**, particularly old people who receive **pensions** from a government.

To be allowed to receive a **pension**, people must have contributed money to it for many years.

What will you do when you grow old?

HOW WILL YOU PAY FOR WHAT YOU WANT WHEN YOU ARE OLD?

5. Keeping Money

5.8 Saving Money

Not spending. Why do it. What is it for.

> **Saving** is level-headed money management.
>
> People who **save** are not wasteful. They are penny-wise, prudent, economical, thrifty.
>
> **Saving** is simply being careful with your money. It is keeping something for future use. To **save** is to put aside, economise, salt away, store, be frugal, horde.

 A miser is an extreme saver:

a person who stores-up money while living frugally /cheaply and being stingy or close-fisted.

Sensible **saving** is not miserly.

You never know what the future will bring — SAVE just in case...

Save as much as you can in the good times, so that you'll then have some financial security for any bad times ahead.

"Savings" refers to money that has been kept for some time in a bank.

Saving up is keeping a little money each week or month, steadily putting it somewhere safe so that you will not spend it (such as in a bank). Gradually bit-by-bit it mounts up. If you save up a lot you can buy something expensive, *without* borrowing.

In this way **saving** can prevent you from getting into debt.

To **scrimp and save** means that you live on a small amount for quite a long time so that you can keep money for something special, such as your education or a holiday.

Trust Funds

People who have saved money sometimes want to give it to others.

A **trust** is a legal arrangement in which a person or organization controls property and/or money for the benefit of another person or organization.

A **trust fund** is an amount of money which is looked after for the benefit of someone, or of an organization, by other people. Some people set up **trust funds** for children, because they are too young to understand how to take care of money sensibly.

Educational trusts are amounts of money kept by responsible organisations that give or lend money to students, for their education, if they fit certain conditions.

A **trustee** is a person, often one of a group, who controls property and/or money for the benefit of another person, or for an organization.

6. Losing Money

6.1 Debt and Credit

Debt is *not* the same as debit. It isn't even similar.

The 'b' in **debt** is silent. It is not pronounced.

> # To owe money is to be in debt
> Not a good thing oh-oh!

Debt is money owed by someone to someone else; usually to a financial institution [bank, building society or loan company]. A **debt** is created when a loan [credit] is given.

Debts cost extra money that is charged by the lender for the privilege of letting people borrow. These charges are called interest.

An overdraft is a kind of **debt** that is owed to a bank.

Creditors are people, organisations or companies to whom money is owed.

Credit is a kind of debt. It is a method of paying for goods or services after you have got them. It is a loan, repayable with interest, offered by shops and financial institutions. If you pay with **credit**, you pay the cost of what you buy, plus, you usually must pay interest too.

"Consumer **credit**" is shopping with a credit card, or store card, and is a way of borrowing money for a month to pay for things.

"Bank **credit**" is overdrafts and loans.

"Trade **credit**" operates between companies that do business with each other.

National **debt** or "public **debt**" is the total amount of money that is owed by a country's government.

Credit terms are the arrangements made for giving **credit**, such as the amount of money, and the period of borrowing.

A **credit squeeze** or **credit crunch** is a time of economic difficulty when it is difficult to borrow money from banks.

A **credit union** is a not-for-profit organisation that is entitled to provide a service to a restricted group of people. Normally they give cheaper loans to employees of a particular company.

THINK TWICE

BEWARE – although *credit is a kind of debt*, that is, a negative thing, it can also be a positive thing, because:

You can **credit** your bank account by depositing money in it.

When you **credit** your account, the bank is holding your money for you, thus registering its **debt** to you. If your account is "in **credit**" it means that it is *not* in **debt**.

debtor	BUT	**creditor**
someone who owes money		someone to whom money is owed

THINK TWICE

It is easy to get deeply in **debt**,
but it's VERY VERY difficult to get out of **debt**.

See section 3.2 on interest. It shows how interest grows, and if you are paying back a **debt** with interest, your **debt** can quickly grow and grow and grow...

...bigger

...and bigger

...and bigger

...and bigger

There is no way out of paying your debts

6. Losing Money

6.2 Default

To **default**, in money terms, means failing to pay back a debt, on time, as legally required. To be *in arrears* is to be late paying what you owe.

A **defaulter** is a person who does not pay back money that s/he has borrowed, as has been previously agreed. If people **default** on loan payments, they will loose the thing that they are failing to pay for.

This failure creates bad credit records for the **defaulter**.

Repossession

Repossession means to take back possession of something that has not been wholly paid for. There are legal procedures that MUST be gone through before property can be **repossessed**. Official notice is given.

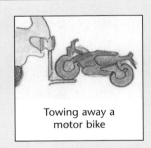

Towing away a motor bike

If you have partly bought something, but cannot finish paying for it, then it can be taken away from you, after a series of official steps – that is, **repossessed** by the person or business that was selling it to you.

Anything that has not been completely paid for can be **repossessed**, even if it is very nearly paid for. It could be a bicycle, a car, a TV, a DVD player, a house... The owners are the sellers: shops or companies. They employ people to take back things that still belong to them.

If people do not pay their mortgages on time, then their houses can be taken away from them by the lender of the money – **repossessed**.

If you buy something using instalment plans or hire purchase remember that you do NOT own it until you have paid the entire price. Until then the seller still owns it, that is, it is still their possession. If you have not continued the agreed payments, then the company that sold it to you has the right to remove it, that is, to take it back, or **re-possess** it. This right is dependent on official notice being given in advance. It is called a **repossession order**. The people who **repossess** property are called debt collectors.

6. Losing Money

6.3 Loss

> **Loss** is the opposite of profit. **Loss** happens when a business spends more money that it earns.

Lost down the drain

Cheap beans

A **loss leader** is a marketing tactic. It is used by large supermarkets.

Items are sold very cheaply, so cheaply, that supermarkets make a **loss** by selling them, but do so deliberately, so as to attract customers into their shops, hoping that they will buy more things and more expensive things while in the shop.

A **loss adjuster** is a person who works for an insurance company deciding how much money should be paid to people who claim for insurance after something has been damaged or lost.

Bad debt

> A **bad debt** is a debt that has little or no prospect of being paid back.

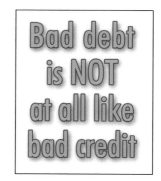
Bad debt is NOT at all like bad credit

Although some unscrupulous lenders encourage people who will never be able to pay back their debts to borrow money – so that they can charge interest, few people would choose to lend money to anyone who is unlikely to be able to pay it back, so **bad debts** are usually unexpected. Occasionally a **bad debt** is forgiven, as a humanitarian gesture or because it's too expensive to collect.

For example, if a country is suffering from drought, epidemic sickness, poverty and war it will not be likely to be able to pay the interest on the National Debt, let alone pay back the debt itself, which, after serious discussion by the lenders and their bankers, *might* then be regarded as a **bad debt** and as a result may be written off. **Bad debts** are debts that will cause more trouble and money to collect than they are worth, or, in extreme circumstances, are simply impossible to collect.

To "write off" a **bad debt** is to cancel the obligation to pay it back. It is VERY RARE INDEED that a debt is written-off, and virtually unknown with personal debts. A very solid and extremely unusual reason would be required. Personal debts *will* be collected – expect it.

THINK TWICE

BEWARE – A loan is *not* a present. Debts MUST be paid back.

6. Losing Money

6.4 Debt consolidation

Debt consolidation is a kind of loan. It is a way of moving borrowed money. It combines many existing debts from various different sources, such as credit cards, overdrafts or other loans, into one large debt.

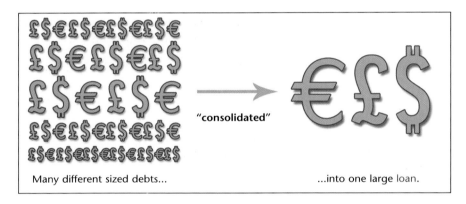

Many different sized debts...   ...into one large loan.

Debt consolidation loan companies pay back all your existing debts, and/or *transfer outstanding balances* (debts) into one debt. The resulting larger debt, is, in many cases, likely to be greater than the sum of all the other debts put together because of high interest rates and charges. In return for combining all your debts into one, you pay back your debt to them, at *their* interest rates.

For some debtors it is simpler to pay back one debt each month, instead of several different debts because each separate debt may have a different rate of interest and some people find it easier to work out their finances on one debt, in order to manage their personal finances each month.

Although each existing debt may have a different rate of interest, BEWARE, that one single debt is *bigger*, and, conditions attached to it can be severe, such as secured loan rules or late payment and management fees. REMEMBER, it will take a longer time to pay off *one larger debt*, because the payments will be spread out over more years.

There are several different possible deals for **debt consolidation** that can be worked out and agreed, depending on how much you earn, your ability to pay debts back, the amount of risk that the loan company thinks it is taking on, and, whether the loan is a secured loan or an unsecured loan.

THINK TWICE

BEWARE...

– Don't be fooled into thinking that **debt consolidation** offers an easier way to pay off debt. It is just a kind of balance transfer. It MOVES debt.

– **Debt consolidation** does NOT make the debt disappear. It still has to be paid; therefore, do NOT take on any more debts.

– There could be penalty fees for paying back your existing debts early.

DOUBLE BEWARE...

– Some **debt consolidation** loans could carry *more* interest than the separate debts combined, making your debtor situation even WORSE.

6. Losing Money

6.5 Debt collectors

A **bailiff**, **sheriff's officer** or **debt collector** is an official who takes away someone's possessions if they cannot pay their debts.

It is a **debt collector's** job to collect unpaid debts from people. If the debtor cannot pay, then the **debt collector** will remove things, the value of which is equivalent to the amount of money owed.

Debt collecting agencies, are companies that are employed by financial institutions that lend money [banks, building societies, loan companies] to go to your house and take away your things: repossess them. They take things that can be sold to pay your debt; usually electronic items such as TVs, fridges, cars, which have about the same value as the amount of money you owe, but cannot pay. Several things can be removed at the same time.

They cannot remove things until a final demand has been sent to you demanding that you pay what you owe. See section 7.1 about bills.

THINK TWICE

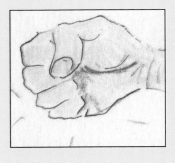

Debt collectors can be very tough

BUT

There is no way out of paying your debts.

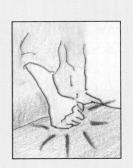

6. Losing Money

6.6 Credit referencing/ checking organisations

Credit Checking organisations ask about peoples' financial backgrounds.

Financial investigators

Credit checking organisations are agencies that, for a fee, will find out the financial history of anyone or any company, and write a "credit report". They charge for their services. You can pay for a "personal credit report".

They can find out whether someone has defaulted on the payment of a debt and whether they have a bad credit history, so that you can then use that information to decide whether someone is likely to pay back money that they borrow. They can also find out whether a company has gone bankrupt, or if they have no information about someone it indicates that it is likely that there is no bad debt or history of not paying on time.

This is a way of finding out whether someone, or a company, that you are not sure about, is likely to be dependable financially. That is, are they really who and what they say they are...? ...or... are they dishonest...?

Some of the main ones are:

– Equifax
– Experian
– Callcredit
– Busibody
– Dun & Bradshaw

REMEMBER – Ask how much credit checking services cost.

Scrutinise information

?????????????????????

6. Losing Money

6.7 DOs and DON'Ts of debt

What to do if you get into debt

Do do do

- Admit it. (It can be hard to face up to)
- Cut up your credit cards
- Talk to your creditors (the people you owe money to). You might be able to arrange a delay in paying back what you owe, or, they may agree to you paying back a smaller amount each month over a longer time.
- Make a list of how much you owe to whom. Prioritise which to pay first.
- Work out very carefully *why* you got into debt in the first place. Be thorough and truthful with yourself. Take a long hard look at your spending habits.
- Reduce your spending. Cut out all things that you don't *really need*, yet allow yourself one *cheap* treat each month.
- Take advice. Search on-line for free advisory services such as: Government Consumer Credit Counselling Services. Make sure to select advisory services that are free of all charges.
- Expect it to require self discipline.

THINK TWICE

SPEND ONLY MONEY THAT YOU HAVE.

£$€¥£$€¥£$

Don't don't don't

- Ignore it. It will *not* go away.
- Try to hide it from close family members. They will inevitably find out.
- Get more credit cards.
- Continuously transfer outstanding credit card balances back and forth between credit card companies. Transferring a debt only moves it, and does NOT pay it back.
- Accept loans from loan sharks or any lender that charges high interest.
- Take out any more loans of any kind.
- Rely on getting extra work or overtime pay.
- Rely on winning or inheriting money. It is not a realistic way to cope with debt.
- Leave nothing to live on.
- Pay for advice. You can get it free, from debt managing organisations.
- Expect it to be easy. Paying off debts can be difficult and take a long time.

THINK TWICE

DEBT – Being in debt is a sad and sorry state to be in. It can soak through every part of your life, dominate your thoughts, and steal your dreams.

Your name is forever on a bad debtors list, which will limit your chances of being able to borrow any money ever again.

Debt may affect your employment possibilities since some employers do not want people who cannot handle their personal finances.

It may also sap your confidence and restrict your chances of success with the opposite sex because many people do not want partners who cannot manage their own money: think it through – you won't be much of a prospect if you are in debt.

So... live within your financial capabilities. Do not overspend.

HELP IS AT HAND

Although debt may feel completely overwhelming and sometimes seem impossible to get out of, there is hope. Do not be downcast. Do not suffer alone. Seek help.

There are *free* **debt counselling services** in most developed countries, many are government sponsored services. Search on the web for: National Credit Advisory Services, a National Debt Line or Consumer Credit Counselling Services.

Credit and Debt Counselling Agencies are organisations that advise people how to cope with and get out of debt. Sometimes they are called "Debt Management and Counselling Services".

Reliable recognised **Credit and Debt Counselling Agencies** set up a programme for you to follow to start paying off your debts.

If you *do* get into debt, don't wait for it to be brought to the attention of debt collectors who will certainly find you; instead, as soon as possible, get professional advice. Sometimes banks offer advice – ask them.

Don't Despair, help is available

Sources of help, advice and information about debt in the UK

Advice UK – UK network of advice providing organisations www.adviceuk.org.uk

Advice NI – General advice and agencies in Northern Ireland www.adviceni.net

Citizens Advice – Independent advice on debt, and on your rights in general. www.adviceguide.org.uk and **Citizens Advice Scotland** www.cas.org.uk

Consumer Credit Counselling Service – A charity that offers free, confidential debt counselling, debt management help, budgeting advice and advice about dealing with creditors. www.cccs.co.uk

Financial Services Authority (FSA) – Mainly a regulatory service, but also has some advice for people with mortgage trouble. www.fsa.gov.uk

National Debtline – Gives a lot of information, plus a free and confidential, independent advice on how to deal with debt. www.nationaldebtline.co.uk

Money Advice Scotland – Tells where to contact free, impartial, independent and confidential money advisers locally. www.moneyadvicescotland.org.uk

Payplan – Free and confidential advice about Debt Management Plans. BEWARE – if you accept one of their Debt Management Plans, you may have to pay for it. www.payplan.com DO NOT PAY FOR HELP

Shelter can give advice on rent arrears www.shelter.org.uk

Tax or VAT arrears – Contact your local HM Revenue & Customs (HMRC) tax office to negotiate paying tax arrears; also try their helpline. www.hmrc.gov.uk

UK Government Information about Public Services – Search on this site under "money tax and benefits/managing debt" www.directgov.gov.uk

---

These organisations exist to provide skilled advice.

DON'T HESITATE – ASK FOR HELP

THINK TWICE

BEWARE of commercial companies pretending to offer free advice when really they want you to pay – so that you get into even more debt.

DO NOT PAY FOR HELP

6. Losing Money

6.8 Bankrupt and Insolvent

"Broke" means having no money, or, in-the-red, cleaned-out, penniless, on one's uppers, down & out, skint, ruined, bust.

Sometimes people joke that they are **bankrupt**, meaning that they haven't got much money,

but,

truly being **bankrupt** has a legal status that involves a petition by the **bankrupt** or by creditors, in a court of law, and has very serious consequences.

Bankruptcy is a legal term for businesses that have totally run out of money. If a company is declared **bankrupt**, then courts of law have the legal right to take control of all the business's finances, and can sell all of the business's possessions to pay the debts.

THINK TWICE

Bankruptcy is not an easy way out of debt. It is a legal procedure that is grim, severe and difficult. It is the last resort.

NOT GOOD

not good at all

not at all good

Bankruptcy and **insolvency** are extreme, life-altering and usually personally disastrous. They are far more serious than merely being temporarily broke, or low on funds. You lose everything you own to pay your creditors. **Bankruptcy** or **insolvency** will be on your credit history for a very long time.

Being **insolvent** is not the same as being **bankrupt**. Individual people, not companies, can become legally **insolvent**. Legal **insolvency** can also happen before a person or company puts forward a formal legal petition to the **Bankruptcy Court**.

A person is **insolvent** if debts are greater than assets. It is a very serious situation to be in, and may affect a person's whole financial life forever.

Courts of law *can* take away everything that an **insolvent** person owns in order to pay back their creditors, even your house. You will be allowed to keep a few basic things required for survival, such as some clothes.

An **IVA** [Individual Voluntary Arrangement] is an arrangement that can be made with creditors to pay back money that is owed by a person who is legally **insolvent**. Not everyone who owes money is eligible to apply for an **IVA**. There are strict rules, one of which is that you must be earning a regular income. If the debtor fits the required conditions, then arrangements may be made to spread the debt that is owed, over several years. Many countries have government help-lines and free advisory services that will advise about setting up **IVAs**.

THINK TWICE

BEWARE – It is not necessary to pay for advice about **IVAs**. **IVAs** are legally binding arrangements, and not the same as **Debt Management Plans**.

Debt Management Plans are sometimes called *payment plans*. They are arrangements, or strategies to pay back money that is owed, that are set down with advice from debt management companies.

THINK TWICE

BEWARE – Companies that advertise their advisory services on TV and on the web are *not* free. They are trying to make money. Do not pay for advice about Debt Management Plans. There are reputable companies and government sponsored services that give free advice. Make sure you go to a licensed debt management company, or better still never need their services.

REMEMBER
All debts *must* be paid

6. Losing Money

6.9 Fraud

Fraud is the crime of gaining money or other benefits by trickery or deceit. It is done on purpose. It's not a mistake or an accident. It is deliberate deception.

A person who is a **fraudster** is someone who gets money by deceiving people. A **fraudster** is a cheat and a liar who does so in order to fool people into giving away their money. It is another way of robbing.

FRAUD:
cheat, swindle, con, dupe, trick, deceive, bamboozle, take advantage of

Fraudulent behaviour is illegal. It is being dishonest on purpose.

You can be **defrauded** by telephone, in shops, by businesses, on web sites, by email... there are many ways that criminals will try to cheat you.

The Fraud Squad is the department in the police that investigates and takes action against **fraud**, particularly business fraud.

If you suspect **fraud**, tell the police. Telephone your local police station, not the emergency number. Find the number in the 'phone book.

Something false or fake is a **fraud**.

Fraudsters will try to cheat you out of your money, so you must be careful to protect yourself as much as possible.

THINK TWICE

BEWARE – **Internet fraud** is becoming more common.

Never give your Financial Identity to any website. If you are paying for things over the net, remember the padlock symbol that, if closed, shows that the site is less likely to be open to **fraud**.

See sections:

6.10 on-line fraud.

6.11 scams.

6. Losing Money

6.10 On-line fraud

There are many ways that crooks try to cheat people on-line.

THINK TWICE

To avoid being caught by these criminals: NEVER, *never* give your telephone number or address to a chat line, or put it on a social networking site, and never put it in an email. There might be someone online who is not really who they say they are...

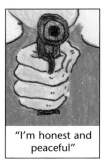

"I'm honest and peaceful"

"I'm not going to rob your house"

"I'm a girl of 17"

BEWARE – People could be pretending to be someone else.

You don't know who a stranger could be. Perhaps it might turn out to be a kidnapper, a pervert or an armed robber!

So, to avoid people who might be dangerous; NEVER agree to meet a stranger – ever. Even if someone sends you a photograph, it could be of a different person. Do not send your photograph. It is part of your personal identity and is private. It can be used to steal from you. Risks of revealing too much information on-line can be electronic as well as physical.

If you chat on-line, *never* give your address, telephone number or real name. Unknown people might be cheats, falsely claiming something, just to defraud you.

Do not even tell people the district where you live, because each small piece of information can gradually be put together to find out who you are and where you live, then if criminals find out that for example you will be out at a certain time, perhaps, when you come home, your house will have been robbed!

See section 6.11 scams

Phishing

Phishing is sinister, not at all like "fishing".

Phishing is the name for the way that criminals try to get private information, such as PINs, passwords, credit and debit card numbers and bank account numbers by claiming to be a trustworthy honest person or business that really needs to know that information. These criminals try to trick people by making their requests for information seem proper and correct, BUT they are not. They will use any means to try to fool you into giving away private information, such as email, chat rooms, social networking sites, text-messages and official looking letters.

If you get an email that seems to be from a bank asking you to "verify your account number" do not give it. If you are asked to "confirm billing information", or, are sent news that you have been "specially selected" for a €10,000,000 prize and just have to fill in your bank account details – don't do it. It is an attempt to steal your financial identity. It's a scam.

Phishers send spam emails that have links to false websites on them. If you click on the link in the email, you will be directed to one of the false websites. They look very good and are difficult to tell from real web-sites. They seem like real bank websites and will ask for your name, address and other private information. It is possible to buy anti-**phishing** technologies.

THINK TWICE

REMEMBER – *Real banks NEVER ask for information on-line.* Don't give away any information. It is a scam.

REMEMBER links in emails may not be safe. For this reason NEVER click on a web-site link in an email. Instead, if you want to visit a financial website, you will get to the real site by writing the web address in the web-address bar at the top of the screen, in the normal way.

Pharming

Nothing to do with agriculture!

Pharming is the name for the technical way that crooks link real web-site addresses, to false web-sites, sometimes called "spoof" web-sites. Computer hackers – who are criminals – redirect the web-traffic from the real web-sites to their false web-sites, usually using a link through spam emails.

Do not visit web-sites that warn that "server certificates are invalid". They are scams.

THINK TWICE

These false websites pretend to be financial web-sites, such as for banks or loan companies. They "phish", by stealing computer users' passwords and by asking for financial information, such as PIN and account numbers. Do not give any.

They are trying to steal your financial identity. It's a scam.

Anti-pharming technologies are now available, but be aware of spoof web-sites. They are scams.

Buying on-line

Do not buy things that you see advertised in emails that came to you un-requested. These "spam" emails can have links to false websites, both as purveyors of computer viruses and of gatherers of your private personal financial identity.

The only time that it is OK to give your name, address and telephone number is when you are buying something from a *well known company* on the net. If you aren't sure whether the company is reputable, don't buy from them. A good test is never to buy from a web-site that does not have an ordinary full postal address; a PO Box number is not good enough. Generally, real companies do not use PO Box numbers, they have proper street addresses.

THINK TWICE

Never buy anything from a web-site unless there are clear policies for security or there is a padlock symbol in the bottom right corner of the screen. The padlock indicates that the site has an electronically secure way of noting your credit/debit card number.

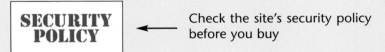

SECURITY POLICY ← Check the site's security policy before you buy

See section 7.9 money on-line and section 8.1 moving money about using postal orders to pay when buying on-line.

6. Losing Money

6.11 Scams

A **scam** is a con-trick.

> Liars, cheats
> DOUBLE-CROSSERS

Dishonest people will try to trick you out of your money, or to use you so that they get something.

> ### Also Known As [AKA]
>
> hoax, sting, ruse, ploy, fleece, fiddle, rip-off, dodge, swindle, diddle, racket, ruse, blag, feint, device, gambit, manoeuvre, scheme, cheat, devious stratagem for gain.

Scams are constantly changing. New ones are being invented all the time, so you have to know what to look for:

> ### THINK TWICE
>
> BEWARE – Anything that sounds as though it is too good to be true, IS too good to be true. In other words, it is a **scam**.

Fraudsters have many methods of trying to cheat you of your money.

There are many kinds of scams. All are attempts at theft. Some common types are:

Pyramid schemes

There are lots of different kinds of pyramid **scams**. All will claim to promise at least these two things:

1. a financial return based on the number of people you are able to recruit to join the scheme.
2. any money you make, will depend mainly on the continued introduction of new members to the scheme and not the sale of a particular product or service.

Pyramid schemes are illegal in many countries, because consumers are too often misled by claims about the likely financial returns. The only way to earn money is by recruiting others into the scheme, therefore those near the bottom of the pyramid *always* find that it is not possible to make the advertised return on their investment.

There are simply not enough people to support a pyramid scheme indefinitely. As a result, usually only the people who set up the scheme are able to make any money.

Pyramid selling, sometimes called *ponzi*, is not quite the same as multi-level marketing because it doesn't involve the genuine selling of goods or services.

If you see a diagram like this in any of the promotional material you receive, then it is a pyramid scheme. Don't touch it. It's a scam.

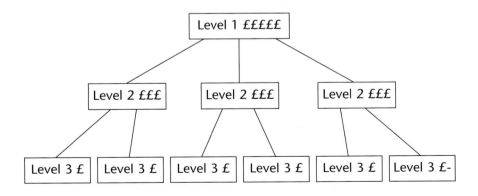

Employment from home / work at home scams

Junk emails, advertisements in the situations vacant pages of daily papers, in internet newsgroups, notes on lampposts or car windscreens, and elsewhere offer incredible employment opportunities... the ability to work from home, at your own pace, and still make loads of cash. It *is not* true.

If you send money or reveal your credit card details it is probable that you will lose your money, and it is unlikely that you will ever hear from the company again. Don't do it, especially if there is no street address but only a PO Box number.

They might ask you to fill envelopes or process emails. Even if you do receive material from the company, it will *not be possible* to make the financial returns promised. These schemes often are similar to pyramid schemes. Steer well clear of them. They are **scams**.

Chain scams

Chain letters and chain emails are similar to pyramid schemes, except they don't always ask you to send money. Chain emails can contain computer viruses. Do not open them. Add them to your "junk senders" list.

Some are just nasty, for example they threaten recipients with bad luck if they don't pass it on. They are complete nonsense. Throw them away. Don't think about them at all. They're **scams**.

Betting scams

Usually you are asked to buy software, that is expensive, which is said to enable you to predict the outcome of horse races, card games or lotteries.

No such thing exists. It's a lie. It's a **scam**.

Clairvoyant scams

Usually these are letters or emails claiming that you have been specially selected to receive advice from a famous psychic or clairvoyant, revealing the secrets of wealth, success and happiness.

Sometimes they even include threats of bad luck if you do not do so-and-so. Lucky charms may also be promised. Ignore them. They'll ask you to send a small fee in order to receive your fortune. Don't do it.

You will not get anything back, and might also get your Financial Identity stolen too. It's a **scam**.

Investment schemes

These so called "opportunities" to invest are presented as though they are legitimate investments. You need to know what to look for:

- does the rate of return seem too good to be true? If so, it *is* too good to be true!
- are the documents provided real? If you aren't sure, don't do it.
- were you telephoned out of the blue by someone who wants to sell you an excellent opportunity to invest? No such "opportunity" exists. Don't do it.

Think about it...how likely is it that an investment advisor, who you do not know, will suddenly decide to telephone you?

What they are trying to do is get your money for themselves.

Even if they tell you that your money will be held in a trust account, or that you will have access to their records, or that they don't have access to the use of your money, *don't do it*. It's a **scam**.

If you decide that you want to invest in something, instead go to a registered Financial Advisor for advice and get a lawyer to look over contracts before you sign.

Invoicing scams

Fraudulent bills are sent in letters or by emails for goods or services that you have not ordered. These are sometimes called "pro-forma invoices" and are illegal. Sometimes the false bills claim to support a charity or a worthy group. Don't respond to them and don't pay them. They are **scams**.

Lotteries and prize draw scams

Fraudsters get lists of names and addresses from electoral registers, telephone books or buy address lists from junk emailers. Once on their lists letters or emails can arrive regularly. You will be promised fabulous prizes, and be told that you are guaranteed to have won, BUT... you'll be asked to pay a "small administration fee". If you pay, you will never get your "fee" back and certainly never get a prize, and you may get your Financial Identity stolen too. They are illegal. Don't do it. It's a **scam**.

If you want to enter a lottery go to a place that is registered and licensed to sell state lottery tickets. If you want to bet, and it is legal in your country, go to a registered betting office.

Mail order scams

Mail order, either from catalogues or on-line, can be a really great and safe way to buy, especially when ordering clothes from reputable well known companies, BUT there are also mail order scams. To reduce the risk, look for:

- large and well-established firms.
- A written statement of money-back if not satisfied. Look at the returns policy.
- A physical (street) address and a contact phone number. Never buy from a company that gives a PO Box number only and no address.

Advanced fee scams

Also known as "Nigerian Scams". One variation of an investment **scam** that's been widely publicised comes from Nigeria, and more recently, South Africa as well as other from countries.

Letters or emails, often addressed to you by name, claim to be from top officials in the Nigerian or some other government who want help to move millions of dollars from a business deal. They say they only want your bank account number and in return promise to make you a millionaire. Do not give them any information. They want your Financial Identity so that they can cheat you, and, if you pay the "advance fee" or "processing fee" that they will ask for, you will never see them or it again. You will lose your money. Don't communicate with them. It is a **scam**.

If they were honest, they would move their money in normal legal ways. See section 8.2 Moving Money Internationally.

Prime bank schemes

These are false investment schemes. Fraudsters claim that there is a secret international market in "prime bank" instruments and that you can get guaranteed high returns by trading these instruments. It is not true.

> Not true
> Not real
> A Fraud

There is no such market. You might be invited to put your money into a trust account, backed by a guarantee (fake) from a so-called "Prime Bank", "Top 100 World Bank", or "Top 25 European Bank". There are no such banks. They don't exist. They claim that your money will be leveraged to buy "prime bank instruments" which can be traded for very high returns. There are no such things. In fact, your money will be stolen.

You may be asked to pay a "promoter fee" in return for a promise that you will be "leased" a much larger sum of money to invest in "prime bank instruments" at fabulous interest rates. There is no such thing. Promoters then disappear taking your "fee" with them. Don't pay. It's a **scam**.

Vanity publishing scams

These are schemes where people are encouraged to have their own writing published, at their own expense. If the publishing company is well known and offers a contract that you can take to a lawyer, it is just possible, though unlikely, that some of these might be legitimate.

BUT... some are more devious, telling people they have been specially chosen, or they run literary "competitions" where the winners have to pay to be published. Avoid publishing schemes asking you to send money. Don't send any. It's a **scam**.

If you want to publish your writing approach well known legitimate publishers or literary agents that handle similar types of writing to yours, or, write a web-blog.

Telephone scams

Fake phone calls – "phake foning"

Fraudsters telephone and ask for information. For example if a woman answers they claim to be doing a survey and at some point ask whether you have got a dog, and whether there is an adult male present. If the answer is no, they may try to rob you later. You don't have to answer survey questions. Just politely say that you are not interested in responding, or, that all personal information is private, and hang up. If they keep on calling you, contact the police.

NEVER give out account details, PINs or other personal information over the phone or by email, especially if *they* have rung *you*. No legitimate company will ever ask you to do this.

Sometimes fraudsters claim to be from a bank and ask you to "confirm" your PIN number or your account number – NEVER give it. It is a **scam** and the fraudster intends to rob you. *Real banks do not telephone you to ask for this information.*

Do not give any information about your Financial Identity, even if they say they are from your bank.

Sometimes fraudsters say that they are from the telephone company and ask for your account number – do not give it. It's a **scam**. The fraudster intends to use your account number for his telephone calls. *Real telephone companies never telephone to ask for this information.* It is different if YOU ring your bank.

Credit card scams

There are many ways to take money illegally from credit and debit cards. Do not let them out of your sight.

Don't hand them to people to swipe unless you can see your card at all times.

They should be swiped *once only*.

Swiping twice could mean that you are charged twice for the same thing. Or, swiping a card a second time on another machine could mean that your financial identity is being recorded for theft later. It merely takes a second or two to swipe a card, so a moment's inattention could result in you being a victim of financial identity robbers.

Occasionally the swiping doesn't work, so use a sensible balanced approach – if someone openly says that the card will not go through a swipe machine properly and tries again in front of you, it does not necessarily mean that fraud is being attempted... but might, as cheats will claim that it didn't work the first time.

Ask yourself:

– what are you buying?
– are you are in a reputable shop?
– are you visiting a website with a security padlock on screen?

THINK TWICE

Always shred or burn your old credit card bills, cheque book stubs and receipts, before throwing them away. They contain all the information a thief needs in order to steal your financial identity. Robbers could find your receipts in rubbish bins, and use the financial information on the old receipts to steal from you in the future.

6. Losing Money

6.12 What to do if you are robbed

In case you are robbed, take these precautions *before* it happens.

Make a note of the emergency telephone numbers which all banks have for reporting lost and stolen bank cards and cheque books. If you do not have the number with you when you are robbed, telephone Directory Enquiries to get it.

After you are robbed:

First:

If your credit or debit cards or your cheque book have been stolen, call the emergency lost and stolen number *immediately* to invalidate them.

Do this as soon as possible. Don't delay even for a minute because thieves will try to use stolen credit and debit cards and cheques, as soon as they steal them.

Second:

Telephone the police. Don't hesitate, don't delay, do it right away.

Tell the police exactly what was stolen from you, when and where. If possible describe the thief as accurately as you can – don't exaggerate, just tell the police exactly what happened, and answer their questions as clearly as you can.

Ask for a "crime reference number" which will allow you to claim on your insurance policy.

It is surprising how shocking an experience it is to be robbed. It can be really upsetting. Take a few deep breaths so that you keep calm.

Once you have reported the theft to your bank, and to the police, it can help to tell your family or friends about it.

THINK TWICE

It is important to report theft. You may not be the only person who has been robbed, and your report might help the police catch the thief. If you notice a thief attempting fraud or stealing – tell the police; it is your responsibility as a citizen to do so. If you see unexplained amounts of money being removed from your bank account, don't assume that you

Help the police to catch thieves

have forgotten about something, it might be an attempt at fraud. Tell your bank immediately; they will investigate and, if necessary, inform the police.

6. Losing Money

6.13 Gimmicks

A **gimmick** is a thing that has little real value and is not serious. **Gimmicks** are used to attract peoples' attention to something else. They are publicity grabbing gadgets, stunts or objects that are usually things of poor quality.

Gimmicks are used to try to make people buy things. For example, breakfast cereals sometimes offer **gimmicks** such as brightly coloured plastic animals, or other small trinkets. **Gimmicks** do not have any long term importance. Some **gimmicks** are stratagems – clever tricks and dodges – that can have a "catch".

It is part of the business of banks, building societies and loan sharks to lend money. They make money by charging interest on money they lend. Therefore they will try to persuade as many people as possible to borrow money. They have a lot of experience in doing this and use highly sophisticated marketing techniques to entice customers into their lending schemes.

As soon as you are legally old enough to borrow money, inevitably you will be sent "offers" about borrowing money.

Remember their offers are to lend money. If you take-up such an offer you HAVE TO PAY IT BACK, plus interest. Sometimes the glossy information does not even use the word "borrow" and highlights only the benefits of getting money without drawing attention to the downsides of borrowing and how much interest you will have to pay for the "privilege" of borrowing. Each brochure might seem more wonderful than the next, but:

THINK TWICE

BEWARE – When banks offer interest "free", it does not necessarily mean obligation free.

Often the time span of the interest free offer is short, after which the interest rate may automatically be HIGH. You may be obliged to keep an account open, and active, for a number of years. "Active" might mean that the account rules state that you must have a minimum balance or a minimum amount paid in each month. Some start-up student bank accounts offer such interest free overdrafts, BUT they might lock you into other commitments, such as paying-in a set amount each month, or may require a minimum flow of money through the account each month; or, may oblige you to keep the account in credit over a certain amount for several years, or, never to let it lie dormant. There are a few good deals, BUT, *read* the small print in agreements to open bank accounts.

BEWARE – "minimum" balance amounts can be quite high.

THINK TWICE

REMEMBER – An "interest free" purchase that spreads payments over some time, is likely to be more expensive than buying something by paying the whole amount immediately.

This doesn't mean that you should ignore good deals. Just take a moment to assess for yourself whether the deal they offer really *is* a good deal, and really is what YOU want.

BEWARE – Some shops offer 10% off first purchase, but only if you continue to buy from them each month. Some banks give away discount vouchers for buying books in student shops, but only if you keep a bank account in credit for some years.

- Ask questions.
- Look for the "catch".
- Check whether an "advantage" might be a disadvantage to YOU.
- Inquire into the details.
- Verify what is required of YOU.
- Investigate your options and obligations.
- Make sure that you know exactly what you are committing yourself to.

A hook to catch you!

If it sounds too good to be true...
...it *will* be too good to be true!

6. Losing Money

6.14 Financial Identity

Not fingerprints

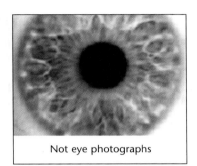

Not eye photographs

Not DNA

But... your **FINANCIAL IDENTITY**

> **Financial identity** is private information that is yours only, and nobody else's. It is unique. It proves that you are you, and not someone pretending to be you. It is very important because you use it to withdraw your money from your bank account(s).

Financial identity information consists of PIN numbers, bank account numbers, credit or debit cards, credit and debit card receipts from things that you have bought, and bank statements, dates of birth, addresses and telephone numbers, all of which are very useful to fraudsters.

Each bank account has a separate **financial identity**.

If somebody else knows your **financial identity** they could rob you.

You must be VERY careful to protect your **financial identity**.

If it is stolen, the robbers can spend your money without you knowing, until it is too late. If the thieves put YOU in debt by spending YOUR money, YOU still have to pay that debt. They pretend to be you; it is called **identity fraud**.

THINK TWICE

BEWARE – NEVER **NEVER** throw out any financial information without first cutting it up into little pieces, shredding it, or burning it. Get into the habit of destroying all **financial information** before throwing it away. Choose a criss-cross shredder that turns bank statements and receipts into confetti, rather than one which cuts to strips which can be reassembled by thieves, who might look through things that have been thrown out in rubbish bins/ trash cans.

Another way for thieves to rob you of your **financial identity** is on the internet. Never trust email. It can be read by other people.

The most common fraud is carried out when people buy things over the internet.

No matter what web-sites claim, ALL sites can be hacked.

The least unsafe method of buying over the internet is to make sure that you go to reputable well known sites. Look for a small icon/ picture of a padlock at the bottom right corner of the computer screen. The padlock sign shows that the company has paid to use a "secure payments site". If you do not see the padlock sign, DO NOT give your credit or debit card details without checking the site's Security Policy.

The risk of **financial identity** being stolen when buying on-line is HIGH, therefore, some people prefer to use postal orders to buy things from internet sites.

Information about **Financial Identity** is so important, that several other parts of this book give more hints and tips about how to keep your money safe.

Refer to security advice in sections:

2.2 bank accounts
2.3 Account numbers
2.7 PIN numbers
2.8 debit cards
3.7 credit score
3.13 credit cards
5.4 end of month financial reckoning / Budgeting
6.9 fraud
6.10 on-line fraud
6.11 scams

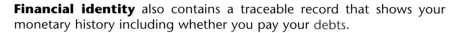
Guard your identity

Financial identity also contains a traceable record that shows your monetary history including whether you pay your debts.

Identity Fraud happens when thieves steal your **Financial Identity**, then cheat while pretending to be you. Criminals do this by using your name, address, bank account number, PIN number, credit or debit card, social security number or passport. They get into debt, but YOU have to pay the debt.

Financial identities are stolen so that criminals can get things or services without paying for them; instead they cheat you, so that YOU pay for them.

It is probable that victims won't know that they are victims until they begin getting bills for things that they know they did not buy, or, until they are refused when they apply for a loan. Even though you are not responsible for the fraud, you may have a damaged credit history, and it can cost a lot of money and a great deal of time to regain your **financial identity**.

Identity Theft Protection

Several companies offer insurance for **identity theft protection** which costs about £50 to £70 a year. They monitor credit reports, alerting customers by text message if anyone is attempting to tamper with or steal their identity. Remember to assess carefully exactly what insurance companies offer, and for what price.

If theft is detected, the insurance offers about £10,000 to go towards the cost of reclaiming your **financial identity**.

There is a victim of identity theft every few seconds.

6. Losing Money

6.15 Money Laundering

Money laundering is illegal. It is a way that criminals try to move money, usually cash that they have got illegally, into a legal bank account. It is sometimes called "cleaning dirty money", or "washing money". They want to claim to police that the money is not illegal.

Money laundering scams work like this. Criminals pretend to make friends with you, then ask you if you will "help" them, "as a favour", or they might even offer to pay you a small amount, if you allow them to put their money into your bank account for a short time and then take it out again. Do not allow it. Say "no". It is against the law.

If you work in a place where cash is handled, people may ask you to exchange large notes for smaller denominations. If this happens frequently, even if it is not the same person asking to change notes, be alert that a group may be trying to **launder money**. Tell the police if you are suspicious.

THINK TWICE

BEWARE – If you do allow it, YOU could go to prison.

Even though they might seem to be nice people, they are not. They are dishonest, and are trying to use you. These crooks try to move money that they have got illegally, perhaps from drug dealing, into a bank account so that they can then move it to their own bank account, and in this way claim to police that it is legal money.

THINK TWICE

REMEMBER – *You* are legally responsible for any money that goes in and out of your bank account, no matter where or who it comes from. It is against the law to let anyone move their money through your account. Don't do it.

---

6. Losing Money

6.16 Gambling

Gambling is a risky act or venture.

Betting on the outcome of games of chance; is chance, just chance and only chance.

There is NO sure way. NO special system. NO secret code. You will NOT get rich.

It is a bet on chance: a speculation, a hazard, a peril.

Owners of **gambling** casinos try to pretend that **gambling** is glamorous, so that people will **gamble**. Some people are fooled into thinking that it is cool to gamble, BUT then they lose their money, which is in no way cool.

Knife throwing:

"safer" than gambling?

Losing money is NOT cool

Think about it – if the owners did not try to make gambling seem to be attractive, who on earth would want to give away their money just to play a game?

Anyone who **gambles** has to realise that they are likely to lose ALL the money that they bet. If you have money to give away, or some spare money to spend, then you'd better realise that's what you are doing by **gambling** – giving away or spending your money in order to play a game. It you don't think it is worth spending your money on a game, then don't **gamble**.

In other words, the owners of the **gambling** web-site, casino, slot-machine, betting office/shop, gaming house ALWAYS *always* make money, BUT **gamblers**, though they may from time to time win a bit, lose more, and never make as much money as the owners of the **gambling** licenses. If owners of **gambling** places didn't make money, they wouldn't be in that business.

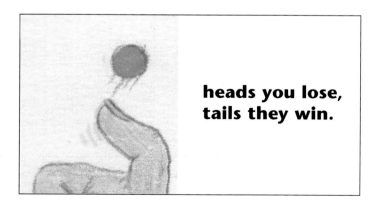

heads you lose, tails they win.

Superstitions, such as crossing your fingers, will not help.

Bookies / bookmakers are people who take money for bets from **gamblers**, especially on horse races.

On-line **gambling** has to be paid for in advance using a debit or credit card.

It is very high risk. Spread-betting is the *most dangerous* kind of betting because before you start you have to agree to allow future losses – debts that you have not yet got – to be recovered from your credit card if you lose, and, it is easy to lose a lot of money very fast. With spread-betting you can even lose more money than you have, which would put you into major debt: MASSIVE debt that could *RUIN YOUR LIFE.*

7. Paying Money

7.1 Bill

invoice, account, note of charge, reckoning, score, statement, tally

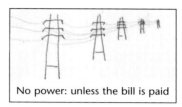

No power: unless the bill is paid

> A **bill** is a request for payment of money owed, for goods or services that you have already got or used.

Utility bills: These are **bills** for services, such as electricity, gas, water and telephones.

Bills for each service are sent to your address. In some countries **bills** are sent monthly and in others, quarterly [= each ¼ of each year] that is, every 3 months.

A utility **bill** looks something like this:

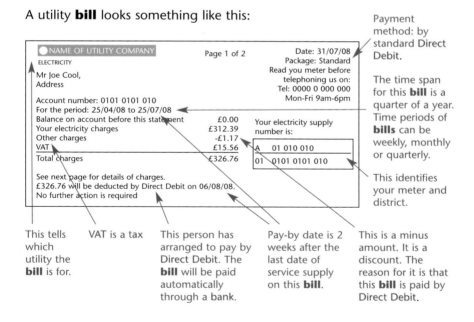

Payment method: by standard Direct Debit.

The time span for this **bill** is a quarter of a year. Time periods of **bills** can be weekly, monthly or quarterly.

This identifies your meter and district.

This tells which utility the **bill** is for.

VAT is a tax

This person has arranged to pay by Direct Debit. The **bill** will be paid automatically through a bank.

Pay-by date is 2 weeks after the last date of service supply on this **bill**.

This is a minus amount. It is a discount. The reason for it is that this **bill** is paid by Direct Debit.

The example bill is paid by Direct Debit, so there is no demand for payment. This bill tells you how much your bank will send to the electricity company, and, the next part gives an itemised explanation of your bill.

If you don't pay by Direct Debit or Standing Order, the bills will have a "due by" date written on them, others print "to reach us by... date". You MUST pay within the time stated. You can pay by sending a cheque, or telephone using a credit or debit card, or on-line. Some post offices and banks accept cash payments of utility **bills** if you take the bill and form on bottom of it with you.

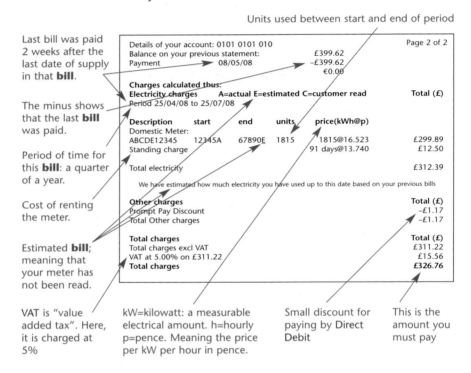

Units used between start and end of period

Last bill was paid 2 weeks after the last date of supply in that **bill**.

The minus shows that the last **bill** was paid.

Period of time for this **bill**: a quarter of a year.

Cost of renting the meter.

Estimated **bill**; meaning that your meter has not been read.

Details of your account: 0101 0101 010					Page 2 of 2
Balance on your previous statement:			£399.62		
Payment	08/05/08		–£399.62		
			€0.00		

Charges calculated thus:
Electricity charges   A=actual E=estimated C=customer read   Total (£)
Period 25/04/08 to 25/07/08

Description	start	end	units	price(kWh@p)	
Domestic Meter:					
ABCDE12345	12345A	67890E	1815	1815@16.523	£299.89
Standing charge				91 days@13.740	£12.50
Total electricity					£312.39

We have estimated how much electricity you have used up to this date based on your previous bills

Other charges		Total (£)
Prompt Pay Discount		–£1.17
Total Other charges		–£1.17

Total charges		Total (£)
Total charges excl VAT		£311.22
VAT at 5.00% on £311.22		£15.56
Total charges		**£326.76**

VAT is "value added tax". Here, it is charged at 5%

kW=kilowatt: a measurable electrical amount. h=hourly p=pence. Meaning the price per kW per hour in pence.

Small discount for paying by Direct Debit

This is the amount you must pay

The next page of the utility bill looks like this:

You must pay **bills** within a certain time, called "pay-by" date. If you do not, you will be sent another **bill**, called a "further demand" or "second demand", and if you do not pay that, you will quickly be sent a last **bill**, called a *"final demand"*.

A final demand bill is usually written in red.

If you do not pay a final demand, your service will be cut-off, and it will not be reconnected until you have paid the **bill**, PLUS a reconnection charge.

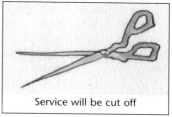

Service will be cut off

If you have not paid the *final demand* utility **bill**, the service company may recover their money from you using debt collectors. In some cases utility service companies have the right to remove an amount from your salary each month until your debt has been paid.

Invoice

An "invoice" is a formal detailed itemised **bill**, usually from a business.

It looks something like this:

It is possible to arrange to pay regular invoices by Direct Debit or Standing Order, if services are used often. In this case, it is expected that the invoice will be paid either immediately face-to-face, or, within 2 weeks by post or with a card over a telephone. You can pay with cash, cheque, credit or debit cards.

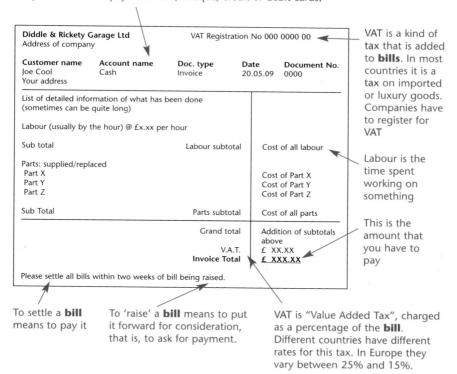

VAT is a kind of tax that is added to **bills**. In most countries it is a tax on imported or luxury goods. Companies have to register for VAT

Labour is the time spent working on something

This is the amount that you have to pay

To settle a **bill** means to pay it

To 'raise' a **bill** means to put it forward for consideration, that is, to ask for payment.

VAT is "Value Added Tax", charged as a percentage of the **bill**. Different countries have different rates for this tax. In Europe they vary between 25% and 15%.

In many countries **bills** should be paid within 2 weeks. In others, you must pay within a month. If you do not intend to pay by the 'due date', you must discuss it with the people you owe, who may not like delays because they have expenses for other things, and may have their own **bills** to pay.

Pay-up

Pay the bill

REMEMBER – You have already got or used what the **bills** are for. You owe money.

A "tab" is an arrangement for paying a **bill** that has been agreed in advance, usually in a club or a bar, that allows the amount owed to mount up over the course of an evening, week or month.

The tab **bill** is paid at the end of the agreed time.

North American English uses some words differently from British English. In North America:

– a "tab" can also mean the total money charged in a restaurant for food and drinks.
– to "pick up the tab/ check" means to pay the **bill**.
– a bill in a restaurant is called a "check".
– a bill is a piece of paper money. $10 bill.

In British English paper money means a note: £10 note.

A restaurant **bill** looks something like this:

The Delicious Food Restaurant
10 Clean Street, Tasty Town

	£
Sesame toast x2	xx.xx
Smoked Salmon	xx.xx
Tomato and Mozzarella Salad	xx.xx
Lamb cous-cous and blackcurrant	xx.xx
Beef Stroganoff	xx.xx
Green vegetables	xx.xx
Chocolate surprise + ice-cream	xx.xx
Apricot moose + cream	xx.xx
Bottle red wine: Cab/Sav	xx.xx
Lime juice	xx.xx
Coffee + mints	xx.xx
TOTAL	xx.xx

Service not included
Thank you

This means that **you** have to calculate how much to **tip**

THINK TWICE

REMEMBER – Before you pay restaurant **bills**, look through them to make sure that they are correct.

7. Paying Money

7.2 Tax

Everyone has to pay **tax** – everyone. It is money that is paid to the government of the country in which you are resident. The amount is calculated based on income or of the goods and services bought.

indirect taxes
are **taxes** on things that you buy or use, not on what is earned.

Sometimes they are called "hidden taxes" because the **tax** is part of the price of the thing that you buy, and is not directly aimed at any group in a population. Anyone who buys the things that are indirectly taxed automatically pays the "hidden" tax.

In most countries indirect taxes are charged on luxury goods or on imported goods, for example, VAT in the UK and most of Europe.

direct tax
the money that a person must pay to the government themselves, such as income tax, rather than through someone else

PAYE
people who are employed usually pay tax "at source" meaning that their income tax is deducted automatically from their salary before they get any. Employers must subtract the required amount and send it to the government. In Britain this system is known as "PAYE" which stands for Pay As You Earn.

tax cuts
are reductions in taxes.

before/after tax

the amount of money you have before/after you have paid tax on the money you earn

inheritance tax

a tax paid on money or property you have received from someone who has died

capital gains tax [C.G.T.]

tax on the profits made from selling something you own

tax allowance

the amount of income on which you do not have to pay tax

tax-free

If something is tax-free, you do not pay tax on it.

council tax

is a UK local government tax that every household in the UK must pay.

tax credit

a sum of money that is taken off the amount of tax you must pay

tax avoidance

the reduction, by legal methods, of the amount of tax that a person or company pays

tax evasion

ways of illegally paying less tax than you should. Tax evasion is against the law.

tax relief

the system of allowing someone not to pay tax on a part of their income

tax return
a form that a self-employed person must fill in to give information about how much they have earned in a year

financial year
A Financial Year or "Fiscal Year" is not necessarily the same as a Calendar Year.

Different countries have different dates of Financial Years.

Some businesses choose to run their corporate accounting years from April till March.

Financial Years for tax do not necessarily start on January 1st and finish on 31st December.

In the UK the financial year starts on April 6th and finishes on April 5th. In some countries it is from July 1st to June 30th.

withholding tax
money taken from a person's income and paid directly to the government by their employer

tax-deductible
If a sum that you spend is tax-deductible, it can be taken away from the total amount of income you must pay tax on.

VAT, Vat
Value-Added Tax (= a type of tax in European countries which is paid by the person who buys goods and services)

VATable
describes goods on which VAT has to be paid:
The rich spend more than the poor on VATable goods.

"...in this world nothing is certain but death and taxes."

– Benjamin Franklin

184

7. Paying Money

7.3   Cash on Delivery [C.O.D.]

Cash on Delivery is a system of paying for things when they are delivered. Usually it is used for business to business deliveries.

Sometimes when things are delivered to your house, the person who delivers it asks to be paid.

COD is not common and is becoming rarer.

THINK TWICE

BEWARE – Do not pay C.O.D. for anything that is delivered to your house unless you are sure that you have ordered it.

Get a receipt.

7. Paying Money

7.4 Discount

> A **discount** is a reduction in the cost of something. To **discount** means to deduct a specified amount or a percentage from a usual price

Sometimes shops offer a percentage (%) **discount** on some items, so as to encourage people to buy more, and to entice shoppers into their shops hoping that once inside, shoppers will buy other more expensive items. If there is no profit for the shop then these reductions are called Loss Leaders.

Discounted goods are those that are cheaper than usual. Reducing the regular cost of something is supposed to encourage shoppers to buy more things. Marketers hope that because shoppers have bought one thing that is cheaper, they'll feel as though they are saving money, so might buy others things and thus may spend more money *overall*.

Going down

Shops sometimes advertise **"discount sales"** meaning that certain items are being sold at reduced prices. Often they are items that could not be sold at normal prices because they are of poor quality.

Usually discounted thing have to be paid for in full immediately and cannot be returned if they are later found not to be suitable.

A **discount rate** is the amount by which goods are reduced in price.

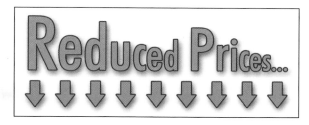

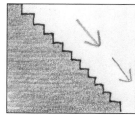

7. Paying Money

7.5 Standing Orders and Direct Debit

Standing Orders are not quite the same as **Direct Debits**, though they are similar.

Both can pay companies by transferring money
from your bank account
to the bank account
of the organisation you are paying

Direct Debit – DD

A **Direct Debit** is a service that is provided by banks or building societies that you can choose to set up. It is an arrangement for paying organisations regularly, directly from your bank account. For example: to pay rent, subscriptions to organizations such as sports or arts clubs, or for paying life insurance policies. Payments can be made weekly, monthly, quarterly or yearly.

To set up a **Direct Debit** you give your instructions to the organisation / company that you want to pay. They will ask you to fill in a **Direct Debit** Instruction form, either on-line, in person or over the telephone. If you do it by telephone you will be sent written confirmation of the **DD** instruction. Keep it for your records. The company that you have instructed will then pass it on to your bank. Note: Not all companies offer **DD**. The **Direct Debit** Scheme assesses companies before accepting them into their scheme.

The company that you pay can collect varying amounts depending on how much your bill is.

People choose to use **Direct Debit** to pay bills because:

- It's convenient.
  Once the **Direct Debit** instruction has been set up, bills are paid automatically and you don't have to do anything, other than keep records of your expenditure. This saves time and effort, and it means that you will not be late paying these bills.
- Many companies, especially utility services, offer discounts if their bills are paid by **DD**.
- It is possible to arrange to spread costs of some bills over an agreed time. This must be agreed in advance with the company that you are paying.
- You are debited at the same time as the company is credited.
- You are protected by the **Direct Debit** Guarantee which entitles you to an immediate refund from your bank if a mistake has been made. Before they collect money from your bank account, companies must tell you how much you are paying, each time your **DD** is paid, so that you know how much will be collected, when, and how frequently, from your account. The company sends a letter or bill, to your address, that tells you this.

To stop a **DD** instruction, tell your bank and also inform the company you have been paying.

The company that you are paying by **DD**, such as an electricity provider, is sure of being paid on time.

If you want to query anything, get in touch with the company you are paying first, then, if there are still questions, ask your bank.

REMEMBER

- Be aware of the date when the DD is due to be paid because you must make sure that there is enough money in your bank account to pay it.
- It is important to know how much you are spending through Direct Debit. Keep the information you are sent when you set up a DD - for your monthly budgeting.
- Although money is collected regularly from your bank account by companies that you pay through DD, the amounts taken may vary each month, especially with utility bills.
  Some companies will let you spread the cost of heating in winter over a longer time. Ask.

Standing Order – SO

A **Standing Order** is another service that is provided by banks or building societies that you can choose to set up. It works in a similar way to **Direct Debit**. It is also an arrangement for paying organisations regularly, directly from your bank account, except:

To set up a **Standing Order** you give your instructions directly to your bank or building society, *not* to the company you are paying. Your bank will ask you to fill in a **Standing Order Mandate**. Your bank then sends your money to the company that you are paying. You tell your bank how much to pay, how often and to which bank account. If you want to change the amount you pay, you have to tell your bank. In this way you have control over the amount that is paid, not the company that you are paying.

People usually use **standing orders** for regular payments, once a month, quarterly [every 3 months], or once a year. You tell your bank how much money you want sent from your account and where you want it sent to – that is – to whom or what organisation, at which bank, what account number and how frequently.

You can ask your bank to set up a **standing order** to anyone or any company that has a bank or building society account. Banks usually take a few working days to complete **standing orders**. Most banks do not charge for this service, but some do. Ask yours.

7. Paying Money

7.6 Insurance

To **insure** means to protect yourself against risk of something terrible happening by regularly paying a special company that will provide a  fixed amount of money if you have an accident and are injured, or if your home or possessions are damaged, destroyed or stolen.

When you insure something you get an **insurance policy**, which is a written agreement between an **insurance company** and you, that states the rules of the agreement.

There are lots of different kinds of **insurance**:

house insurance
Depending on how much you pay, and what you agree with your insurers, sometimes this kind of insurance will pay for repairs to roofs or accidental damage to household goods, or even for the whole house to be rebuilt, but the monthly payments would be very high for that.

credit and debit card insurance
It is possible to **insure** against the theft or loss of credit and debit cards, but may not be worth it, because customers are not at present liable for fraudulent use of bank cards IF, and only if, they inform the bank of theft or loss of cards *immediately*, the moment they know about it, though BEWARE: this may change in future.

national Insurance
is a social insurance system in Britain, financed by tax contributions paid by employers and by employees. It provides payments to unemployed, sick and retired people.

health insurance

This kind of **insurance** is for paying for private medical treatment, and for money to live off in case you become disabled so that you cannot work. You have to make regular payments to an **insurance** company in exchange for that company paying for most or all of yourmedical expenses. In many countries there are government health insurance programmes, and or free or partly free treatment for tax payers.

job insurance

If you **insure** against loosing your job, you have to pay each month for all the years that you work in return for which, *if* you loose your job, you receive regular monthly payments to cover your mortgage and other costs, after you stop work.

car insurance

of which there are several kinds, for example:

– **comprehensive insurance** for a car which financially protects any other vehicles and people that are involved in a car accident with you, in addition to yourself.

– **third-party insurance** will pay money for damage caused to someone by the person who has this insurance

travel insurance

These vary a lot. Most cover loss of or damage to luggage, sickness and various other things. It depends how much you pay. Look carefully through the terms and conditions.

life insurance or life assurance

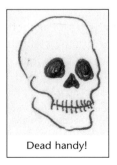

Dead handy!

Of course after you are dead you can't get any insurance! – but your family can. If you make regular payments to an insurance company, a fixed amount of money will be paid to someone you have named, usually a member of your family, when you die.

term insurance

is a type of insurance which lasts for a limited time period.

7. Paying Money

7.7 Tipping

Tip, gratuity, service charge

A small amount of money given for a service rendered, beyond the agreed-upon cost.

Waiters rely on **tips** to supplement their wages.

Usually tip
10% – 12% of the bill

Tips are paid in addition to the bill. It is an "extra", on-top-of the bill.

Tips are expected, and usual, in restaurants, but not required.

Some restaurants write on their bills "Service not included" as a way of trying to encourage people to **tip**. *You* decide how much you want to **tip**.

Rarely less than 10% never more than 15%

If the waiter has been extremely efficient and very well mannered you might want to thank him/her by giving about 12% of the whole **bill**.

If s/he has behaved normally, but not exceptionally, you should **tip** 10%.

Occasionally for really perfect service you may choose to give more, perhaps 14%. Even more rarely, if service has been very slow, bad mannered and sloppy, you may decide not to **tip** at all [that is, 0%], but you may not be welcome there again!

Tips on tipping

Don't let scowls, fidgeting or grunts bully you into giving more than YOU want to. It's *your* money. You decide what to do with it.

When you leave a **tip**, do not put it on the credit or debit card, instead leave the **tip** in cash. This way the waiters who serve you are more likely to get the **tip** rather than the owner of the restaurant.

BEWARE – If you pay by credit or debit card, ask the waiter to bring a chip and pin key-pad to the table, or get up and go to pay the bill where you can see that your card is swiped only once. See section on fraud.

BEWARE of bills that include service. Sometimes the final total includes service, but you can't tell till you look through the bill. This is a common trick. **Do not pay another tip**. If you aren't sure, just ask, "Is service included?" They won't be annoyed to be asked.

Sometimes restaurant bills do not say what percentage has been added. Work it out, or ask. 15% is too much for ordinary service in Britain – but is done in some places in London – you need not necessarily pay it all, though if you don't, you might get some frowns. You MUST pay the bill, but *you* choose how much to **tip**, and if you want to go back to that place, do leave *some* **tip**.

Other people to **tip**:

- *Porters* who carry suitcases to rooms in hotels, or in railway stations.
- *Hotel maids* – hand it to them or leave cash in the room & lock the door when you leave, so that nobody else can go in and take the money.
- *Cloak-room attendants* – someone who is working hanging-up coats.

- Many people tip *hairdressers*; some do not.

In these situations there is no percentage to calculate.

Don't give too much, a few coins, a word of thanks and a smile is just right.

You might want to thank hospital nurses with chocolates, flowers or a bottle of wine, not money, after spending more than a day or two in hospital.

Taxis – most people tip taxi drivers, some never do. In general:

- For short journeys, of up to a few kilometres, it's OK not to tip, but some people do.
- For medium length journeys, say 3 to 15 kms, **tip** up to 10%, or, you could "round up" the bill – if it is £9.42, give the driver £10.

- For long journeys, of over 15/20 kms agree the price in advance, in which case no **tip** is necessary. Make that clear before you start.
- Each country has different conventions for paying taxis.
- Make sure that the meter is switched on, and starts at zero.

7. Paying Money

7.8 Loyalty / reward / advantage / store card

> A **loyalty card** is a plastic card which is given to a customer by a business, often by a supermarket, which is used to record information about what the customer buys, when, where and for how much, and to reward them for buying goods or services from the business.

Supermarket **loyalty cards** are a way for companies to find out your buying pattern and your buying power. **Loyalty cards** collect a vast amount of information about each person who uses them. They are marketing and sales tools for supermarkets. The name for this *gathering of information from private citizens* is "customer profiling". The data they collect tells them much more than merely what you buy and the amount you spend. It tells them how, where and who you live with and what your lifestyle choices are.

When you fill in the application they ask for:

– your name – which can be cross referenced with, for example the voters roll.

– your address – so the shop knows how far you travelled to get to them, so they can judge whether you might be likely to buy petrol; and, can send advertising [junk mail], unless you specifically ask them not to.

– your date of birth – so they can find out what people of your age buy most.

   Dates of birth can be cross-referenced with other computer systems to find out completely unconnected information.

Each time you use a **loyalty card** the shop can tell:

– what date you shopped
– what time of day you shopped
– how you paid – cash, cheque or card
  if you paid with a cheque/debit or credit card they will know which bank you use, and the number of your account
– how much you spent
– what you bought – exactly what – the brand, colour, size and quantity
– what sort of medicines or vitamins you regularly buy, and from that information might guess what your state of health might be

– what kinds of and how much meat you buy; so, if you buy none, they may suppose that you might be vegetarian
– what sort of things you read, so might guess what your politics are
– how much alcohol you buy – telling them whether you might drink to excess.
– where you shop – which shops, in what districts of which towns, so they'll know your routine and occasional routes.

With **store cards** they can follow your trail.

From the information they collect; such as how frequently you buy certain things, they can work out how many people you buy for, what their approximate ages are and what they tend to like. Once they cross-reference all this information, they can also discover other things. For example, if you often buy in a country as well as in a city location, perhaps you have a second home, or frequently visit someone in one of those places, and from this they can guess your likely income, and even your preferred method of travelling and your route [if you buy petrol, where do you buy it, or do you buy things at their shops in railway stations, if so in which?] – and so on.

REMEMBER

All computer systems are hackable!

WE KNOW YA

They are able to spot out-of-pattern purchases quickly. An obvious guess would be if you start to buy nappies regularly that you have a new baby in your family. Using all this collected data, they set up computer programmes that can tell them a very great deal about you. It is perfectly legal.

Loyalty cards let supermarkets find out ALL ABOUT YOU...

It doesn't take much imagination to realise that **store cards** gather A LOT OF INFORMATION ABOUT MANY INDIVIDUAL PEOPLE.

They know all this about *you*, but you know very little about them.

Many people allow all this *detailed personal information to be collected for years* by choosing to use **loyalty cards**.

MONITOR ~ OBSERVE ~ WATCH ~ KEEP TRACK OF ~ SURVEY PRY ~ SPY-ON ~ INTRUDE ~ SCREEN ~ EXAMINE ~ KEEP TABS ON MAKE UNINVITED INQUIRY ~ EXTRACT INFORMATION...

Shops entice people into giving all this private information, by offering some reductions, usually only on perishable good that they cannot otherwise sell, their own brands of goods, or those bought with monopoly or near monopoly buying powers. Some of these shops sell the information they have gathered about you to other companies. If you want to avoid these tracking systems, spend cash when you buy in these shops.

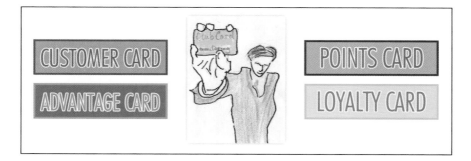

CUSTOMER CARD

ADVANTAGE CARD

POINTS CARD

LOYALTY CARD

7. Paying Money

7.9 Money Online

Some people have 2 debit cards, one with a limit of £200 maximum for use on-line, and one for normal use, that they NEVER use on the web. In this way it is easier to see whether there may have been any fraudulent payments. See section 6.11 Scams.

Risk... Hazard... Chance of loss...

Paying on the net:

Make sure that a symbol such as the safe shopping padlock sign is present in the bottom right corner of the computer screen or that a reputable payment provider is certifying handling the money away from the site.

Some people set up special email addresses to use when buying on-line, so that if an email address gets into the hands of junk emailers, it can be deleted once the purchase is complete. Thus, the possibility of junk email getting to a personal email address is reduced.

THINK TWICE

BEWARE – Debit and/or credit card numbers can be stolen if they are revealed on-line, so *never* email them. PCs can be hacked; so, some people choose to use Postal Orders to pay for goods ordered on-line, rather than risk fraud and identity theft. Postal Orders are safer than any secure on-line purchase sites.

If you shop on-line, one of the safer ways to pay is to use one of the on-line payment companies, such as **Worldpay** or **PayPal** or another well known payment provider. They do not give any financial information to the seller, thus reducing the chance of your financial identity being stolen  and misused. These payment provider companies take money from buyers and pass it to the sellers with comparatively secure electronic encryptions.

They work like this:

When you reach the "checkout" stage on screen, you will see the name of the on-line payment company. Click on it. Then pay using a debit or credit card, directly through your bank, or with a balance that you have already pre-paid and is held by the on-line payment company. Your payment is sent to the sellers' account with the on-line payment company, then, the sellers transfer your payment to their bank account. These on-line payment companies work if you buy or sell through EBay and with some other on-line shops. It works in many parts of the world, though not everywhere. It is possible to buy and sell using different currencies. It is quick.

The on-line payment companies charge the seller a graded / banded / sliding scale according to the amount of money spent by buyers.

THINK TWICE

REMEMBER – Make sure that you read the 'terms and conditions' *thoroughly* so as to know what costs you are liable for

BEWARE – Hackers can break into computer systems of companies and governments. *Everything* on-line is at risk to malicious hackers, who may steal money, financial identity, or destroy data on your computer.

Even the most secure on-line site still contains risk. This does not mean it is not safe to shop online, but do not assume it is always secure. Be alert.

Paying Money

8. Moving Money

8.1 Bank Transfers

You can instruct your bank to move money between your own bank accounts or to someone else's. The accounts do not necessarily have to be in the same bank.

Banks charge for this service. Banks' systems of transferring money are:

CHAPS

CHAPS is the system of UK bank to UK bank same day transfer of money.

CHAPS stands for **C**learing **H**ouse **A**utomated **P**ayment **S**ystem. It is the system of transferring UK£s within the UK between bank accounts. Go to a UK bank and fill in a money transfer form.

Most banks have a standard 7 day service costing a fee of about £18, and an express 2 to 3 day service for a fee of about £20 per transfer.

A set fee of about £25 is usually charged for a same day transfer which is guaranteed only if you get in touch with your bank before 1.30pm, so as to give them time to complete the transfer that same day. Ask how much your bank charges.

CHAPS Euro

CHAPS Euro is the system of transferring Euros inside the UK between bank accounts. Money must be transferred to an individual's bank account.

BACS

BACS is the system of UK bank to UK bank 3 days transfer of money.

BACS stands for **B**ankers **A**utomated **C**learing **S**ervices. It is usually used for transferring large sums of money such as to pay for a house, car or to pay lawyers.

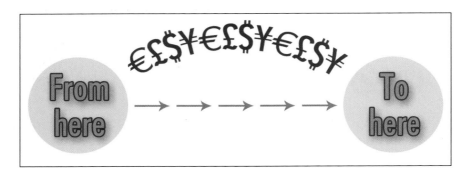

In some countries, new mobile phone technology enables people to move money to and from banks, and to pay for things in subscribing venues and companies.

 **BACS** stands for **B**anks **A**utomated **C**learing **S**ervices. As transactions are not immediate it is often used for payments that are planned in advance. It is usually used to transfer smallish amounts of money regularly, through Direct Debit, Standing Order or to pay salaries with Direct Credit. Internet and telephone bank accounts use **BACS**. Ask your bank how much they charge, though many banks offer **BACS** for no fee.

 **APACS** is the UK payments association for financial institutions that make payments to customers. Through **APACS**, financial institutions can discuss general issues connected with payment systems. **APACS** also airs issues connected with plastic cards, card fraud, cheques, electronic payments and cash."

THINK TWICE

BEWARE – A **bank transfer** is NOT the same as a balance transfer, which is moving a debt.

Fastpay is being introduced by several banks for transferring up to £10,000. Smaller amounts can be sent by **Fastpay** using Standing Orders. It is a bank-to-bank same day electronic payment system that is designed to replace CHAPS. Banks aim to transfer money in "near real time", but guarantee transfers within three days. It is available for internet and telephone bank accounts and soon will be for people who visit banks too. There is no charge to customers.

Postal Orders

A **postal order** [**money order** in North America] is an official piece of paper, of a similar design to a cheque, with a payment amount of money already written on it, in words and numbers. They can be got for amounts up to a maximum of £250.

You *buy* **postal orders [POs]** at post offices. You can ask the post office to print the name of the person to whom you are sending money on the **postal order [PO]**, or, you can write the name yourself. The post office will rubber-stamp it; then you put it in an envelope and send it through the normal mail service.

Then, the person to whom you have sent it, whose name is written on it, takes the **postal order** to any post office, and, once proof of identity is provided, can then exchange it [cash it] for the same amount of money, immediately. 47 different countries use POs, and more will join. If you are not sure that the country to where you want to send or take money uses postal orders, ask at a post office, or look on-line.

Postal orders are a safe way of sending money through the post instead of sending notes/ bills, which could be stolen or lost. **Postal orders** cost less than 9% of the value of the money sent, charged on a sliding / graded / banded fee scale.

Postal orders expire six months after they are issued. You do not need a bank account to buy or cash a **postal order**, unless you get it 'crossed' when you buy it.

THINK TWICE

REMEMBER – Get a receipt for your **postal order**.

BEWARE – Post offices *never* send email receipts for **postal orders**; if you get one, ignore it; it is from a thief who is trying to rob you. See section 6.11 scams.

Some people use **postal orders** for shopping using mail-order catalogues or for buying things on the Internet, because they are safer than using credit or debit cards on-line, thus reduce the risk of identity fraud. Send them by registered mail.

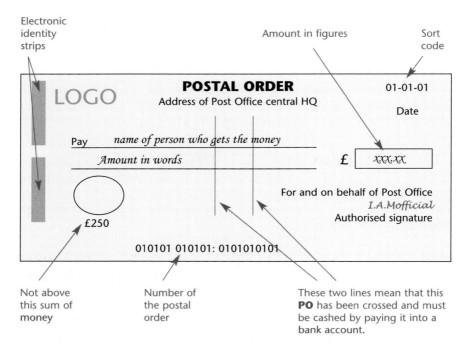

Electronic identity strips

Amount in figures

Sort code

POSTAL ORDER
Address of Post Office central HQ

01-01-01

Date

LOGO

Pay _name of person who gets the money_

Amount in words

£ _XXX·XX_

For and on behalf of Post Office
I.A.Mofficial
Authorised signature

£250

010101 010101: 0101010101

Not above this sum of money

Number of the postal order

These two lines mean that this **PO** has been crossed and must be cashed by paying it into a bank account.

8. Moving Money

8.2 Moving Money Internationally

There are several ways to move money between countries.

Using banks:

— electronic transfer,
— bankers drafts,
— travellers cheques,
— letters of credit.

Or, using:

— International money transfer companies, such as MoneyGram.

Electronic transfer

Electronic transfer or **telegraphic transfer [TT]**, sometimes called **sending money by wire**, **wiring money** or **wireless transfer**, is an electronic system of transferring any currency internationally.

You have to give banks the name and number of the bank account of the person you are sending money to (called "the beneficiary"), plus, the name and address of the bank to which the money is going, and, if within Europe or North America, one of the following:

— an IBAN [International Bank Account Number]
— a SWIFT number which is a message code used between banks so that they can identify each other
— a BIC [Bank Identifier Code] number

Your bank will tell you this information, and it is on cheques.

Electronic transfer is fast, but expensive.

Most banks have 3 types of transfer, depending on how quickly you need money:

> An urgent transfer – same day transfer – the most expensive
>
> A standard transfer – takes about 5 working days
>
> A relay transfer – takes between 7 to 10 working days – the cheapest

Some banks charge using a sliding/graded/banded scale of fees for this service. Others charge a flat fee of about £20 for transfers within one country, and about £25 for international transfers. Ask your bank how much they charge. Take ID to your bank when you go to arrange this.

Bankers' draft

Sometimes called a **foreign draft**.

A **bankers' draft** is a document written by your bank, that can be taken, or sent, to another country and cashed there, BUT **bankers' drafts** cannot be used unless the person to whom you are sending the money, or you, already have a bank account in the country where you want to send the money, or, unless there is an agreement between the banks internationally, known as an "affiliation", or, if there is no agreement between the banks in different countries, then an intermediary bank, which is known to the sending bank, will be used. This bank is known as a "corresponding bank". This allows you to cash **bankers' drafts** from a bank in one country, in a different bank in another country. **Bankers' drafts** can be written to you or to someone else.

Most banks charge around £15 per draft, for any amount, or, apply a sliding / graded / banded, fee structure. Ask your bank how much they charge.

It takes less time to cash a **bankers draft** in the same currency, say a Euro to Euro transfer, than to cash one made out in Euros but collected in UK£ or US$.

Travellers' Cheques

Travellers' Cheques are a quicker, but more expensive way to get your money in another country. See section 9.3 travellers' cheques.

Letters of credit

Letters of credit are usually used between businesses for buying goods. A **letter of credit** is a letter from a bank allowing the person who has it to take a particular amount of money out of a bank in another country. The letter, or document, is issued by a bank and in effect substitutes the bank's credit for the customer's credit. Expect banks to find out about your credit history before they agree to issue a **letter of credit** for you.

It usually works only if the banks in each country have a trade "association" with each other, part of which is an agreement to accept one another's **letters of credit**.

To get a **letter of credit** you have to go to a bank to request it. They will arrange it and charge you for it. **Letters of credit are used for international trade.**

International Money Transfer Companies: Money grams

Another way to move money internationally is through **International Money Transfer Companies**. There are many companies that will transfer money for you. Compare their prices before using their services.

Money grams are a way of sending money internationally. 170 countries have money gram offices. **Money grams** are bought in one country and sent to other countries' **money gram** offices. In many countries **money grams** can be bought in Post Offices, and in others may be bought in a web-café, a fax office or a shop. In the UK **money grams** can be bought at post offices from where they are sent to other countries' **money gram** offices.

The person who sends the money has to go to the **money gram** office to pay for it and fill-in a form that arranges to send it. From some places they can be paid for on-line. The person to whom the money is sent, must go to a **money gram** office to collect it. Identity documents must be shown.

The service takes about an hour internationally.

There is a sliding scale of charges which diminishes proportionately according to how much you send:

Up to £100 costs about £12
Up to £200 costs about £18
Up to £300 costs about £24
Up to £400 costs about £30

and so on till

£5,500 costs about £160

In most countries the limit is about £5,500.

THINK TWICE

REMEMBER – Once the money has been paid out to the person you name as the receiver, cancellation or refund of a **money gram** is no longer possible.

If you intend to pay for goods and services with money from a **money gram** that you expect to arrive, wait a few days before buying, so as to be sure that it has really been paid into your bank account.

THINK TWICE

BEWARE – of attempts at fraud.

Be suspicious if you are sent a **money gram** [or a cheque] with a request that you send some of the money to someone else, even if you know the sender and potential next recipient. Remember that money laundering is illegal – see section 6.15.

The **money gram** is unlikely to be real. YOU could be responsible for the amount of money that you send to someone else, and you will not be able to get the rest of the money – in other words, someone is trying to cheat you into sending your money to a stranger, and you will get nothing.

No reputable companies EVER send emails to confirm or inform a person that a money transfer has been sent to them or paid for an internet purchase. If you get such an email, do not believe it. Even if it contains the **MoneyGram** name and logo, it is a fraud.

International Money Transfer Companies: Western Union

Another of the well known **International Money Transfer Companies** is Western Union.

Western Union is a system of same day international transfer of money. Many countries use this service. Family members use **Western Union** to send money to each other. It is designed for sending money between countries, NOT for buying goods or services.

BEWARE – It *is possible* to use Western Union to buy goods or services from one country while in another, but is *NOT* safe to do so. There are no guarantees, and many people have lost money attempting to buy things that do not exist!

¥€£$¥€£$

Western Union is especially useful for sending money to places that have few banks, or to remote areas. There are limits: of approximately €7,000 / £5,000 / $8,500 every 30 days, sent in a maximum of 3 transactions.

The money is usually paid in local currency, except in a few countries where it can be collected in US dollars or Euros, as well as in local currency. BUT... the fees for this service are not cheap. Fees are charged using a sliding scale; so it is cheaper to send larger sums every two months or so, or even less frequently, rather than smaller amounts more often.

The cost of sending money is paid at the point of sending. Money must be sent to an individual, that is, to a named person, not to a business. The person to whom the money is sent is called the "recipient", and must have an identification document such as a passport, driving licence or ID card, in order to pick up the money, and must know precisely how much money is being sent, as well as the full name of the person who sends the money. It is better if the recipient also knows a 10 digit reference number, unique to each transaction, which is called a "Money Transfer Control Number" (MTCN). The sender of the money must tell **Western Union** what kind of identification document the recipient has.

There are 3 ways to do it:

1. Go to a **Western Union** agent in the country from where you want to send money. Agents can be travel agents, post offices, small corner shops, some supermarkets, certain financial institutions and some banks. You can pay with cash, up to US$1,000 or equivalent in local currency. Larger sums can be paid by credit or debit card or by cheque. Fill in a form, and the agent will send the money on your behalf.

> **THINK TWICE**
>
> BEWARE – Thieves know that people pay with cash, so watch out for robbers.

2. Telephone **Western Union** from a land line.

You will be asked for your name and address, date of birth, and to "nominate" one particular land line telephone number as your contact number. Pay using a debit or credit card. They accept Visa or MasterCard only. Then wait for 4 to 6 minutes, till you are told that the transfer has been accepted. 20 minutes later the money will be available to be picked up by the recipient in the other country.

You have to pay fees...

THINK TWICE

REMEMBER – Find out exactly how much *your* bank charges, before you use these services.

---

3. On-line, by visiting a Western Union website, available in several languages.

Fill in a form of 5 or 6 pages to register, and then telephone the number that is given, so as to validate the transaction. Pay with a credit or debit card.

Again, Visa or Mastercard only. Limits on the frequency and amounts of money that can be sent are slightly higher when paying on-line.

Before you start, look up the countries that you are sending from and to, because some countries do not accept on-line transactions.

9. Money Abroad

9.1 Currency

> **Currency** is the system of money used in any country.
>
> Each country or group of countries has their own kind of money.

If you go to another country you will need to use the **currency** of the country that you are visiting. In order to get the **currency** you need, you have to go to an exchange. Some banks have exchange facilities. Exchange rates change daily, making the amount of **currency** you get for your money vary.

Hard currency is money that has value in lots of different countries because it comes from a powerful country. It is money that floats internationally. You can get it outside the country where it is used, that is, exchange it easily for other **hard currencies**.

Three well known **hard currencies** are:

Euros: €	British pounds: £ UK£ or "sterling"	American dollars: US$

All of these and most other well known **currencies** are internationally exchangeable – or convertible – they are known as **hard currencies**. For example: Japanese yen, Australian dollar, Turkish lira, Jordanian dinar, Mexican peso.

Soft currency is money that you *CANNOT* get outside the country where it is used – that is – it is not internationally exchangeable for any other currency.

Soft currencies have value *only* in the country where they are used. They are of *no use* anywhere else. Examples of **soft currencies** are:

North Korean won, Albanian lek, Ukrainian hyrnvna, Mongolian tujhrik.

THINK TWICE

BEWARE – Watch out for illegal money changers. They are people who change money outside banks, either in the street, or somewhere that the police cannot see them. It is against the law.

Money changers may offer a better rate of exchange than banks, BUT, they may also try to cheat you, or even rob you.

9. Money Abroad

9.2 Exchange Rate

Different countries use different kinds of money, and currencies have to be converted from one to another. The **exchange rate** is the level at which one currency is exchanged for another.

To *float* a currency means that it is allowed to alter against other currencies, depending on global political and economic changes. This is why **exchange rates** change slightly daily. To get a general idea of the value of your money, find out what the **exchange rate** is before you travel. **Exchange rates** are announced in the money sections of newspapers, or, search on the web using the key words "currency exchange", then enter which currencies you want to find out about.

To withdraw money from your account using an ATM of another bank in another country with your normal debit card, you will usually be charged a conversion fee of about 2.75% *PLUS* a service fee of about £2.50 by your bank.

THINK TWICE

BEWARE – Remember that **exchange rates** alter frequently, day to day.

It is easy to make a mistake with the number of zeros in some currencies, so, *before* you go shopping, jot down how much your money is worth so that you can refer to it as you shop.

For example (exchange rates here are for illustrative purposes only):

UK£		Currency A
£1	=	A1.42
£5	=	A7.09
£10	=	A14.18
£20	=	A28.37
£30	=	A42.52
£40	=	A56.72
£50	=	A70.91

Keep it in your wallet or purse

Currency A		UK£
A1	=	£0.70
A5	=	£3.52
A10	=	£7.05
A20	=	£14.10
A30	=	£21.15
A40	=	£28.20
A50	=	£35.25

It will give you a quick reference guide and can be really handy.

THINK TWICE

When you first get new currency, take time to look carefully at it, so that you know how much each note and coin is worth.

In some countries numbers are written differently from in Britain.

For example:

in Britain [the UK] one thousand two hundred and thirty four point fifty six is written like this:

BUT
in some countries, it is written like this:

1,234.56

1.234,56

It means the same, but, notice the different position of the COMMA and POINT.

This can be *confusing* so pay attention.
THINK what you are doing with your money.

9. Money Abroad

9.3 Travellers' Cheques

A **travellers' cheque** is a piece of paper that you buy from a bank or a travel company and that you can use as money, or, exchange for the local money of the country you visit. They can be obtained in several **hard currencies**.

Travellers' cheques are designed to be used in other countries to buy things in some large shops, and, can be converted into other currencies when they are cashed in banks in other countries.

The advantage of **travellers' cheques** is that you can claim the money back if they are lost or stolen, BUT BEWARE – your bank will charge for them, and the bank in the country where you withdraw your money will charge you a flat fee or a percentage for each **travellers' cheque** that you cash.

Travellers' cheques do not look exactly like ordinary cheques, but are similar. They are already printed with precise sums of money. You must buy them in advance from a travel agency or your bank before you travel. When you get them, you must sign each one, then, later, when you use them to withdraw money from a bank in another country [cash them], or to buy goods with them, you must "countersign" them. This means that

you sign again with exactly the same signature, in the place marked "countersignature". Ask whether the bank or shop will accept your **travellers' cheques** *before* you countersign one. *The bank teller must see you sign your* **travellers' cheque**, so do not countersign them in advance. You'll need your passport for identification.

Travellers' cheques are usually available in multiples of ten – that is, 10s to 100s, depending on the currency in which they are written. Any unspent **travellers' cheques** can be converted to cash on your return to your own country, but, REMEMBER that the exchange rate may have changed since you bought them, and you will have to pay bank charges for this service.

Travellers' cheques come with separate pieces of paper for writing a list of the cheque numbers. DO THIS in advance, and keep the list of cheque numbers somewhere separate from the **travellers' cheques**. This will let you claim their value if they are lost or stolen. Some banks charge for sending you **travellers' cheques**.

Also see section 8.2 Moving Money Internationally

Index of Financial Terms

Look for money words and expressions in Chapters and Sections